OSPREY AIRCRAFT OF THE ACES • 64

# Yakovlev Aces of World War 2

SERIES EDITOR: TONY HOLMES

OSPREY AIRCRAFT OF THE ACES • 64

# Yakovlev Aces of World War 2

George Mellinger

OSPREY
PUBLISHING

**Front cover**
**On 24 August 1943, the pilots of Ivan Stepanenko's 4 IAP (Fighter Aviation Regiment) were sitting in their Yak-9s at Bryansk at 'readiness one'. Their orders were to escort a large formation of DB-3Fs from Long Range Aviation which had been sent to bomb an enemy position nearby. The Yaks were to take off when the bombers flew over their airfield and then escort them to the target. But the bombers never arrived. Suddenly, a report reached the base that the bombers had missed their rendezvous point and proceeded to the target without any fighter escort. Now they were being savaged by Fw 190s.**

**Three green rockets shot up at Bryansk and the Yak pilots received the order to take off at once and attempt to defend the bombers. As soon as the fighters took off and gained a little altitude, their pilots could clearly see several DB-3s falling like burning torches, with parachutes descending earthwards. Stepanenko later recalled;**

**'There was no time to assemble the whole regiment, so pilots took off in flights, pairs and even alone, hurrying to battle, regardless of the risk. We threw ourselves directly at the enemy. Intoxicated with their success, the Focke-Wulf pilots were flying as if possessed.**

**'I selected one of them, heavily mottled, and hit him with a burst of cannon and machine gun fire. The fascist turned over on his wing and went down, leaving a thick trail of black smoke in his wake. Then two others drove me down toward the forest, hammering at me with eight cannon. The shells cut through the dark blue sky to the right and left like flaming arrows. Unexpectedly, the surface of my fuselage cracked. "Now, Ivan", I thought to myself, "you've had it". Exceeding maximum G-load, I banked tightly to the left. My eyes grew dark. I released the stick to avoid spinning. I saw two Fw 190s following me into the vertical. I quickly moved into position for a head-on attack so they couldn't get on my tail. I opened fire and, like balls, the enemy fighters broke from me to both sides. Making a reversal and then going into a steep dive, I headed for home, and safety' (*Cover artwork by Mark Postlethwaite*)**

First published in 2005 by Osprey Publishing
Midland House, West Way, Botley, Oxford OX2 0PH, UK
443 Park Avenue South, New York, NY 10016, USA



ISBN 1 84176 845 6

Edited by Tony Holmes and Bruce Hales-Dutton
Page design by Tony Truscott
Cover Artwork by Mark Postlethwaite
Aircraft Profiles by Jim Laurier
Scale Drawings by Mark Styling
Index by Alan Thatcher
Origination by PPS Grasmere Ltd, Leeds, UK
Printed in China through Bookbuilders

05 06 07 08 09 10 9 8 7 6 5 4 3 2 1

EDITOR'S NOTE
To make this best-selling series as authoritative as possible, the Editor would be interested in hearing from any individual who may have relevant photographs, documentation or first-hand experiences relating to the world's elite pilots, and their aircraft, of the various theatres of war. Any material used will be credited to its original source. Please write to Tony Holmes via e-mail at: tony.holmes@osprey-jets.freeserve.co.uk

# CONTENTS

# YAK DEVELOPMENT

The 1930s represented a period of rapid development in aviation technology. Although the Soviet Union's Polikarpov I-16 had been one of the world's leading fighters only three years before, it was outdated by 1939. The USSR's most likely opponents were replacing their Fiat, Heinkel and Bristol Bulldog biplanes with Macchis, Hurricanes and, more importanlty, the deadly Messerschmitt Bf 109E. So in 1939 the Defence Commissariat issued a requirement for a new generation of combat aircraft.

Four proposals for the new fighter were selected for development. Surprisingly, all four were submitted by teams new to fighter design, namely Yakovlev, Mikoyan and Gurevich (MiG), Lavochkin, Gorbunov and Gudkov (LaGG) and Yatsenko. All had started their careers working with Polikarpov and Tupolev.

Aleksandr Yakovlev's team had been assembled in 1934, and had already designed a number of successful trainers and light civilian aircraft. Yakovlev had been sketching plans for a fighter even before 1939, and now submitted four different concepts. One, for a low to medium altitude tactical fighter, was approved in May 1939 and given the designation I-26. The first prototype was completed on 27 December 1939 and flew from Moscow's Central Airfield on 13 January 1940. The aircraft was painted bright red overall with white trim, and since the airfield was covered in snow, it was fitted with skis. The competing LaGG flew on 30 March and the MiG on 5 April. The Yatsenko I-28 had flown as early as June 1939.

The Yakovlev I-26 was a conventional low-wing monoplane of mixed construction. The forward fuselage comprised a steel truss with Duralumin skin, while the rear section was a wooden structure with fabric covering. The wings were of wooden construction and the ailerons, flaps and tailplane were made of Duralumin. The engine was to be the liquid-cooled, supercharged Klimov M-105P V12, which had also been selected for the LaGG competitor. Armament was to be a 20 mm ShVAK cannon firing through the propeller hub and four rifle calibre machine guns mounted in pairs above and below the engine. However, due to weight requirements the lower pair of machine guns was deleted from the second prototype.

From its first flight, the I-26 revealed itself as a potential thoroughbred. Even when the first prototype crashed on 27 April 1940, the decision was made to continue development. A number

**Aleksandr Yakovlev (left) meets 154 IAP ace Pyotr Pokryshev (31 and 7 shared kills) in the spring of 1944 and presents him with one of the first pre-production examples of the Yak-3 (*G F Petrov*)**

**Naval Air Force officer Lt L K Vatolkin of 8 IAP-ChF stands before an early model Yak-1 in Sevastopol in the spring of 1942. Commanding an *eskadrilya* in the first year of fighting over the Crimean peninsula, he is reported to have claimed five kills. Vatolkin's final fate remains unrecorded (*G F Petrov*)**

**Local women help to camouflage a Yak-1. Literally thousands of Soviet aircraft were destroyed by marauding Luftwaffe fighters on the ground in 1941-42 (*G F Petrov*)**

of problems materialised. The landing gear and brake mechanisms were unreliable, and there was a tendency for the Klimov engine's oil temperature to rise excessively, and for it to leak oil. But the I-26 handled well, and was both manoeuvrable and fast. Although the shortcomings were eased by design modifications, they were never completely cured. The Klimov M-105 remained troublesome throughout the war, and similar problems afflicted the LaGG. The impressive performance figures also declined after necessary modifications had been made to strengthen the aircraft's structure and full operational equipment had been fitted.

A first pre-production batch of fighters, now renamed Yak-1, was sent to 11 IAP (Fighter Aviation Regiment) at Kubinka, just east of Moscow. The third prototype continued its development trials. 11 IAP converted onto the Yak-1 without trouble, and by November 1940 the third prototype had also completed its pre-production flight testing. The fighter was approved for service.

During the autumn of 1940 the Yak-1 entered series production at Factory No 301 in Moscow and Factory No 292 in Saratov, where it replaced the ill-starred Yatsenko I-28 on the production line after only five examples had been produced. Factory No 301 discontinued production in 1941 after only 117 Yak-1s had been built, but production at Saratov continued

The Yak-1's short-lived RS-82 rocket installation can be seen beneath the port wing of this unidentified aircraft (*G F Petrov*)

until July 1944, by which time 8550 examples had been built.

The initial production Yak-1 had a maximum speed of 348 mph at 15,570 ft, its service ceiling was 32,500 ft and it could climb to 16,400 ft in 6.8 minutes. The fighter could turn in 19-20 seconds. Its armament consisted of one 20 mm ShVAK cannon and two 7.62 mm ShKAS machine guns. Within weeks of the German invasion in June 1942, pilots found that the 7.62 mm guns lacked penetrating power, and both they and the cannon jammed too often in combat.

In the summer of 1942 the two ShKAS were replaced by a single 12.7 mm UBS machine gun, which saved weight and increased firepower. Early Yak-1s were also equipped with six underwing rails for RS-82 rockets. This weapon was intended for aerial combat, but proved equally useful for ground attack. Ultimately, 1148 Yak-1s were equipped with rockets, but they were removed in May 1942 when it was realised that they created too much drag for fighters engaged in air combat.

Cockpit instrumentation was basic, and most airframes had either no radio at all or just a receiver, with no transmitter. Only by mid-war were sufficient radio sets available to provide all fighters with transmitter-receivers. Many aircraft were not fitted with oxygen equipment, limiting their ability to operate at higher altitudes.

The aircraft also had inadequate armour and fuel cell protection, earning the Yak-1 an unenviable reputation for burning easily when hit by enemy fire. If this was not bad enough for the pilot, the canopy had a tendency to stick when the aircraft was in a dive, rendering escape difficult! For this reason, and also because of the notoriously poor quality of Soviet transparencies, many pilots flew with their canopies open. This resulted in increased drag and reduced speed. With new production batches, these shortcomings were addressed, as armour was provided both for the pilot and fuel system.

A Yak-1 displays the factory-applied early war black and green camouflage scheme, which also featured blue undersides. The pilot in the centre may be Nikolai Mikhailovich Gusarov HSU (Hero of the Soviet Union), who claimed 15 individual and 14 shared victories with 486 IAP during the course of 432 combat sorties (*G F Petrov*)

In the winter of 1941 Saratov manufactured 830 Yak-1s equipped with retractable ski landing gear. One pilot who flew such a machine was future ace Boris Eryomin of 296 IAP. He reported that it was a very unsatisfactory aircraft, being slower than a standard Yak-1 because of the extra weight and drag of the skis, and plagued with a variety of maintenance problems. If a ski happened to fall out of its well during flight either because of combat damage, mechanical failure or even a violent manoeuvre, the aircraft would

A ski-equipped Yak-1 provides the backdrop for a squadron photograph in early 1942. Both the pilots and the unit remain unidentified (*G F Petrov*)

become uncontrollable. Pilots also had to be more careful in landing, since the angle of approach was much less forgiving than with the wheeled undercarriage. Even then, the skis proved particularly vulnerable, and were in continuous need of repair. This may explain why the ski-equipped Yak-1s were never seen again after the winter of 1941/42. Presumably the survivors were sent back to the factory for conversion to standard landing gear.

During the summer of 1942 the Yak-1 underwent several major changes. In addition to swapping its two ShKAS for a single 12.7 mm UBS, the airframe was also modified by cutting down the rear fuselage and installing a bubble-shaped canopy (which greatly improved vision), together with a plate of armoured glass behind the pilot's head. From 1942 the M-105PF engine was installed, and this increased power to 1180 hp and boosted the aircraft's top speed to 366 mph. It also cut the time to climb to 16,400 ft from 6.8 to 5.9 minutes. This version went into production in September 1942 as the Yak-1B, and accounted for 4188 of the 8670 Yak-1s produced.

The Yak-1B proved so popular that several of the leading aces preferred it to the later model Yak-9, which was heavier and less agile. Sergei Luganskii was one of the aces who stuck with the Yak-1 almost until the end of the war.

Another modification was the Yak-1-Lightened. This variant saw the replacement of the wooden tail section with an all-metal unit. Armour and fuel tank protection, radio and all other non-essential equipment was stripped out and both machine guns were removed, leaving only the cannon. This saved 357 lbs of weight, and significantly improved climb. Ten aircraft were sent to a Moscow PVO (Anti-Air Defence Forces) unit in early 1942, and in September another 20 were produced and sent to the Stalingrad front. Flown by an experienced pilot, such fighters could

This rear view of an early Yak-1B clearly show its cut-down rear fuselage. Note that the landing gear doors have also been removed (*G F Petrov*)

compete on equal terms with the Bf 109G-2, although armament and protection were inadequate for average pilots.

In March 1940, even while the Yak-1 was still being evaluated, Yakovlev submitted another design for a tandem two-seat fighter trainer, initially designated UTI-26. It was similar in appearance, engine, dimensions and performance to its cousin the Yak-1, and it also had the same faults and virtues. But it had only two ShKAS machine guns, and was structurally strengthened in a number of places. After testing, the aircraft was approved for production as the Yak-7UTI at Factory No 301, where it replaced the Yak-1. Initially, the Yak-7UTI was assigned to training duties only, but because its performance was comparable to that of the Yak-1, it was decided in August 1941 that the Yak-7 should also be built as a fighter.

This variant featured an armoured backrest fitted to the rear cockpit and fuel tanks protected with an inert gas system. Armament comprised one ShVAK, two ShKAS and six RS-82 rocket rails. The rear canopy was retained so the fighter appeared identical to the trainer, and could carry a passenger during redeployments or reconnaissance missions. In comparison with the Yak-1, the Yak-7's speed was about the same, although manoeuvrability was slightly less. The Yak-7's landing gear,

This Yak-7B was regularly flown by Capt Vladimir I Merkulov of 15 ORAP (Reconnaissance Air Regiment). It is seen here in April 1944 (*V Kulikov*)

The austere cockpit of a production Yak-7 (*G F Petrov*)

which had been strengthened to withstand mishandling by student pilots, also stood up better to the rigours of operational airfields. Spinning and handling characteristics were also superior. The fighter variant of the Yak-7 went into production and the aircraft entered service with 172 IAP in September 1941.

Factory No 301 was evacuated from Moscow in late 1941 and Yak-7 production was shifted to Factory No 153 at Novosibirsk. Its first aircraft were completed in late 1941, and the factory had turned out 4888 Yak-7 variants by the time it switched to other types in 1943. Later in 1942 production was resumed in Moscow, at Factory No 82, which had produced 1320 Yak-7s by 1944. Five more Yak-7s from a factory in Gorkii brought the total to 6399 airframes, of which 277 were Yak-7As and 5033 were Yak-7B variants.

The improved Yak-7A appeared in early 1942, featuring the addition of a radio, mast and aerial, oxygen equipment, a semi-retractable tailwheel and a supercharged engine. The aft-sliding rear canopy was replaced by a side-hinged plywood hood, providing a cleaner rear fuselage. Although slightly less manoeuvrable than the Yak-1, the Yak-7A was marginally faster than early versions.

Attempts to improve the Yak-7A led to the Yak-7B, which boasted a M-105PA engine with increased power, two 12.7 mm UBS guns instead of a pair of 7.62 mm ShKAS and redesigned air intakes which, combined with other measures, reduced drag. Although the Yak-7B was heavier, speed was not decreased, and its weight of fire was 1.5 times higher than the Yak-1 and earlier Yak-7s. Production of this variant began in April 1942, and by late May it had entered service with the famed 434 IAP.

Yak-7Bs of 29 GIAP sit at Uglovo airfield, near Leningrad, in late 1942. Most of the aircraft have had their Klimov engines covered with insulated covers to protect them from the cold (*G F Petrov*)

From 13 June to 3 August, this regiment flew 875 sorties with the Yak-7B on the Stalingrad Front, and claiming 55 victories for only three aircraft shot down. Late series Yak-7Bs were fitted with the cut-down rear fuselage similar to the Yak-1B.

Seeking to improve the Yak-7's armament, the Yak-7-37 appeared in August 1942 with the 20 mm ShVAK cannon replaced by a powerful Shpitalnii MPSh-37 37 mm weapon. These aircraft were sent to Boris Shinkarenko's 42 IAP, operating on the Northwestern Front. The unit was pleased to find that the cannon functioned flawlessly, a hit from a single shell usually being enough to destroy a fighter – it could punch a hole over 10 ft square! Although only 22 Yak-7-37s were produced, thousands of Yak-9T fighters were similarly armed from 1943.

In an attempt to address the problem of range, Yakovlev devised the Yak-7D and then the Yak-7DI. These aircraft featured a new wing construction and greatly increased fuel capacity. The Yak-7DI had a cut-down rear fuselage, and one of its UBS machine guns was deleted. The aircraft was ordered into production, but it was later redesignated the Yak-9.

This new variant continued to use the Yak-7's 1180 hp Klimov M-105PF engine, but improvements in industrial techniques permitted the substitution of Duralumin for much of the wooden structure. This produced great weight savings, as well as better strength. Performance was raised, and armament comprised one 20 mm ShVAK cannon and one 12.7 mm UBS machine gun. The Yak-9's speed was increased to 372 mph at 14,000 ft. Service ceiling was 36,500 ft and climbing to 16,400 ft took 5.1 minutes. The Yak-9 turned in 16-17 seconds.

The Yak-9 went into production at Novosibirsk in October 1942 and entered service in December with Shinkarenko's 42 IAP in the defence of

**Although the pilot walked away from this crash, the damage he had inflicted on his Yak-9 was almost certainly terminal (*G F Petrov*)**

Clothed in typical winter flying gear (including standard dog-fur boots and life preserver), an unidentified pilot known only as Serov stands in front of a Yak-9 from 26 GIAP on the Leningrad Front (*G F Petrov*)

Stalingrad. In January 1943 Factory No 166 at Omsk started Yak-9 production, while Factory No 82 continued turning out Yak-7 variants until early 1944, when it switched to the Yak-9U. By the end of the war 14,579 Yak-9s of various types had emerged, with post-war production to the end of 1948 raising the total to 16,769 Yak-9s.

Only 500 of the original Yak-9s were built before it was supplanted by modified variants, the first being the Yak-9T in which the 20 mm ShVAK cannon was replaced by a 37 mm NS-37 weapon. The latter's 330-lb weight necessitated airframe modifications, and its heavy recoil required considerable structural strengthening. The cockpit was shifted 15.5 inches to the rear but speed was barely affected, while climb and

Again clothed in his winter flight gear, yet another unidentified pilot prepares to take his Yak-9 aloft (*G F Petrov*)

These Yak-9T/Ms of an unknown unit based on the Baltic Front are notable for the broad bands (possibly in red and white) on their spinners. This type of marking was unusual for Soviet fighters (*G F Petrov*)

manoeuvrability suffered only slightly. As the cannon carried a limited number of shells, pilots learned to use the UBS machine guns for sighting, and then to fire a short burst of two or three rounds from the cannon. The NS-37 proved a powerful weapon, needing only two hits at most to destroy virtually any type of enemy aircraft.

The first Yak-9Ts emerged at the end of March 1943 and saw action at Kursk with units of the 16th Air Army. During the test period, from 5 June to 6 August, 34 Yak-9Ts claimed half of the Air Army's 110 victories. Only 12 aircraft were destroyed in return. By comparison, other Yak units lost three times as many aircraft in the same period.

Initially, it was standard practice to issue the Yak-9T to the formation and flight commanders and then pair leaders. Regular 20 mm cannon-armed Yaks were allocated to the wingmen, who had the task of protecting the attackers. The Yak-9T proved one of the most popular variants, 2748 being produced. Later, in 1945, the Yak-9K appeared with

This Yak-9DD from 236 IAD was photographed in Bari, Italy, in the autumn of 1944 while the unit was supporting Tito's partisans in Yugoslavia (*RART*)

an even bigger gun. The 45 mm NS-45 cannon was a very powerful weapon, but the recoil had a devastating effect on the airframe and its weight had a significant effect on speed and manoeuvrability. Production ended after only 53 aircraft.

Although it could be used against ground targets, the Yak-9K's main mission was in destroying bombers, which by then were mainly Fw 190 *Jabos*. Against such aircraft, the 45 mm shell represented sheer overkill – perhaps another reason why the Yak-9K was discontinued.

The Yak-9D series had increased fuel capacity, which extended its range from 410 to 562 miles. This had a serious negative effect on all other aspects of performance, however, and also created a fire hazard, as the extra tanks were not well protected. The Yak-9D was distributed to regiments where it was mixed with other sub-types. The Yak-9D's long range was generally wasted as a result, for the other regimental aircraft could not accompany it for the total duration of a mission. Their degraded performance meant that standard Yak-9s had to fly at reduced speed to avoid breaking formation. Consequently, the Yak-9D was not particularly popular, and many pilots flew with the extra wing tanks left empty. Usually assigned to junior pilots, 2934 were produced.

In 1944 the Yak-9DD appeared and 399 were built. This aircraft carried even more fuel and had a range of 820 miles, but again there was a cost to performance. It is best known for the detachment which flew non-stop from Beltsy to Bari, in Italy, in August 1944, from where they provided air support to Tito's Yugoslav partisans.

Perhaps the most unloved Yak-9 version was the Yak-9B, a bomber variant which carried four 220-lb bombs (or an equivalent weight of 2.2-lb anti-tank weapons) vertically loaded in the fuselage behind the cockpit. Just over 100 were built.

Col Shinkarenko had spent most of the war commanding 42 IAP as a field test unit for Yak innovations, including the Yak-7-37, and the first Yak-9s.

**Although the Yak-9B fighter-bomber variant was not a success, more than 100 were built. This particular aircraft, assigned to 130 IAD, was bought with funds contributed by Moscow's Little Theatre, as noted by the inscription on its fuselage (*G F Petrov*)**

This Yak-9M, photographed in Poland in late 1944, also features spinner decoration in the form of a Germanic spiral. The badge on the nose is the Order of Suvorov, while the inscription reads *s pobedoi!* ('with victory!') (*G F Petrov*)

Now he was assigned to organise 130 IAD (Fighter Aviation Division), together with 168 and 909 IAPs (equipped with the Yak-9B), and 409 IAP with the Yak-9T as escort. From November 1944 they operated over Poland, but without a real bombsight, bombing was inaccurate. Loading the bombs was difficult, as they often got hung up in the aircraft. When fully loaded, the effect on flight characteristics was severe.

Throughout the war poor construction detracted from the theoretical performance of Soviet aircraft, including the Yak fighters. Component parts often did not fit properly, surface finishes were rough and parts were not firmly fastened. There were even cases of old rags being found in the exhaust pipes and tools left behind in the fuselage. One defect played a particularly notable role in Yak history.

One day in the summer of 1943, a Soviet pilot was dogfighting in his Yak-9 when the wing surface peeled away, causing him to crash. Following a series of similar incidents, Marshal Josef Stalin summoned Yakovlev to the Kremlin and ordered him to find the cause and correct it immediately, or be accused of sabotage. An investigation revealed several contributing factors, including a wing of insufficient strength, but also a flaw in the paint. One of the components of the green camouflage paint was in very short supply, and a supervisor in the chemical factory producing it had made an unauthorised substitution in the formula. It had reacted adversely with the glue attaching the wing's fabric covering. The correct formula was restored, the wings were strengthened and repair brigades were sent from the factory to field units. However, by then several hundred Yaks had been lost through incorrectly mixed paint.

Wartime Yak-9U photographs are rare, and these examples could be flying immediately post-war. They do display typical late-war green and grey camouflage (with blue undersides), however, and note that aircraft 9 features a yellow band around its rear fuselage. The bumps ahead of the windscreens on the nearest two aircraft are gun cameras (*G F Petrov*)

**Georgii Baevskii (wearing helmet) briefly flew this Yak-9U in 1945, but soon returned to the La-7 (see *Osprey Aircraft of the Aces 56 - LaGG & Lavochkin Aces of World War 2* for further details). He did not score any of his 19 victories in this aircraft. The nose marking that adorns this machine is striking *(G F Petrov)***

The Yak-9M appeared in the summer of 1944, with a strengthened wing structure, the Yak-9T's rearward cockpit and the Yak-9D's increased fuel capacity. It also had the standard 20 mm cannon armament. A few sources suggest that the Yak-9M also had two UBS machine guns fitted, but there is no compelling evidence to support this. Visually, the fighter's most distinctive feature was its forward-slanted radio antenna. From May 1944, 4429 examples were built.

In November 1943 Yakovlev embarked on a radical redesign of the Yak-9. Numerous changes were made, particularly to the wing structure, which simultaneously lightened and strengthened the aircraft. New water and oil coolers were installed, and the nose scoop was replaced by underwing units. A new spinner and propeller were also adopted, while its armament was increased through the fitment of a 23 mm VYa-23 cannon and two UBS machine guns. Most importantly, a new powerplant was finally provided in the form of the Klimov VK-107A, which produced 1500 hp and raised the fighter's top speed to 417.5 mph at 16,500 ft. The Yak-9U was produced from May 1944, although it took until October to reach the front. It nevertheless made a notable impression on both Soviet and German pilots during the last six months of the war in Europe.

Meanwhile, development of the light Yak-1 had continued, and by late 1943 a highly improved Yak-1M had been tested. This aircraft evolved into the Yak-3, which entered production in February 1944 and went to the front with 91 IAP at the end of June. It featured a number of structural changes in comparison with the Yak-1, including a reduction in wing area. The new Klimov VK-105PF-2 engine developed 1280 hp to produce a speed of 397 mph at 14,500 ft. It climbed to 16,000 ft in 4.1

An unidentified Yak-3 undergoes field maintenance in the spring of 1945 (*G F Petrov*)

minutes, had a service ceiling was 34,000 ft and could complete a turn in 19 seconds. Armament consisted of a 20 mm ShVAK cannon and two 12.7 mm UBS machine guns. In addition to being built at Saratov, Yak-3s also starting emerging from Factory No 31 at Tbilisi – its aircraft were noted for their superior construction. Ultimately, 4848 Yak-3s were built, 937 of them post-war. In the final year of the war in the east the Yak-3 established itself as the best low-level fighter on either side.

By the end of the conflict 32,051 Yaks had been produced – more than any other combat aircraft apart from approximately 33,000 Bf 109s and 36,363 Il-2 *Shturmoviki*. Production of a further 4635 Yak-9 and Yak-3 variants post-war raised the total of Yak propeller fighters to 36,686, making it the most prolific combat aircraft of all time.

The Yak was operated by most fighter regiments and flown by most aces – even those associated with other aircraft. Indeed, Aleksandr Pokryshkin (59 and six shared kills) and many other Airacobra aces flew the Yak-1 for much of 1942. A number of regiments primarily equipped with other types of fighter often operated a few Yaks in one squadron. Another Soviet peculiarity was the habit of mixing different varieties of Yak in a single regiment. This not only meant combining different sub-types of Yak-1, -7 and -9, but also the simultaneous use of the major sub-types. Although this practice seems to have become less common during 1944, as large quantities of Yak-3s and Yak-9Us arrived with their substantially increased performance, it never completely ended, despite the implications for maintenance and formation flying.

There was, though, one peculiarity of deployment. Notably fewer Yak-1s served on the Leningrad and Karelian Fronts, although some Yak-7s operated in Leningrad, mainly with 29 GIAP (Guards Fighter Aviation Regiment). The explanation is that all Yak-1s were produced at Saratov, on the southern Volga. They were much easier to assign in the south, leaving units equipped with Hurricanes and Kittyhawks shipped through Murmansk to face the Finns in the north. For the LaGGs and Yak-7s produced in Novosibirsk, the northern and southern flanks were equidistant. Even so, some Yaks flew with the northernmost regiments.

# EARLY YAK ACES

The first production Yak-1s reached Moscow-based 11 IAP in mid-May 1941, the unit being led by G Kogrushev. This regiment had carried out operational trials of the pre-production I-26 during the summer of 1940, and it was therefore the natural choice to receive early-build Yak-1s. 11 IAP would serve as an informal training/conversion unit to help introduce other regiments to the aircraft.

When the Germans launched Operation *Barbarossa* on 22 June 1941, 425 Yak-1s had been built, although just half that number had actually been assigned to line regiments. Only Moscow Air Defence Region's 11 IAP was completely equipped and operational with 62 Yak-1s, while a further 30 Yaks were shared between other regiments protecting the Soviet capital. In Kiev Special District, Sambora-based 20 IAP had 61 Yaks (together with 60 I-16s and I-153s) for 63 pilots, while 91 IAP had received just four Yak-1s to supplement its Polikarpov biplanes.

In Western District, 123 IAP had recently received 20 Yak-1s to supplement its 61 I-153s. Leningrad District's 158 IAP had 20 Yak-1s, Baltic District had only eight with 13 IAP at Pyarnau, and 20 had been shared between the Baltic and Black Sea Fleets. The remaining Yaks were either being sent, or had been distributed in ones and twos, to individual units. By contrast, 917 MiG-3s had been deployed in the border districts, which meant that relatively few of the valuable Yak-1s were caught on the ground in the Luftwaffe's surprise attack on the morning of 22 June.

**An unidentified pilot poses in front of his Yak-1 for a propaganda photograph in late 1941 (*G F Petrov*)**

On the Western Front, the Yak-1 soon began playing a significant role in the defence of Moscow, with Col Kogrushev's 11 IAP contributing the lion's share of Soviet successes. The regiment's first victory went to Lt Stepan Goshko, who intercepted a He 111 over Rzhev on the night of 2 July. He was flying one of the pre-series Yak-1s at the time, and when his guns failed, Goshko brought the bomber down by ramming it. His aircraft was damaged, but he made it to base. Goshko saw most of his action during the first period of the war, and was fated to survive with a total of six individual and eight shared victories.

As previously mentioned, on the outbreak of war 158 IAP had 20 Yak-1s, as well as some I-16s. Piloting one of the Yakovlevs was Snr Lt Pyotr Afanas'evich Pokryshev, who had twice been shot down by ground fire during the Winter War with Finland in 1939-40.

On 24 June Pokryshev scored his first victory when he intercepted a lone Ju 88, although his own aircraft was shot down by defensive fire. By July 3 he had scored his fifth victory. That autumn Pokryshev

**Pyotr Pokryshev's Yak-7B was put on display in mid 1945 in the Defence of Leningrad Museum. The multiple ace flew this aircraft with 29 GIAP up until the late spring of 1943. Note the Guard's emblem behind the cockpit (*G F Petrov*)**

was transferred to 154 IAP (29 GIAP from 21 November 1942). There, he flew Curtiss fighters until January 1943, when the regiment converted to the Yak-7. On 10 February 1943 Pokryshev became a Hero of the Soviet Union (HSU), and on 10 July shot down the Fw 190 of 40-victory ace Ofw Peter Bremer of JG 54. About a week later he was given command of Yak-7-equipped 159 IAP.

This Yak-7 was assigned to Lt Col Aleksandr Andreevich Matveev, 29 GIAP regimental commander, in the early spring of 1943. During the war he appears to have scored six individual and nine shared victories, in addition to two individual and five shared kills claimed against the Japanese over Mongolia pre-war (*G F Petrov*)

As he flew the short distance to his new unit's base, Pokryshev spotted a formation of Ju 88s. Climbing to attack them from astern out of the sun, he dived downed and destroyed two bombers before the escorts caught up with him. After a brief dogfight, Pokryshev was able to escape by diving away under the cover of fire from Soviet anti-aircraft guns. Soon after his arrival at 159 IAP, the unit received La-5s, which Pokryshev regularly flew until VE-Day. On 24 August 1943 he was awarded his second HSU, but was badly injured soon after during a training flight in a UTI-4.

While Pokryshev was recuperating, Aleksandr Yakovlev presented him with one of the very first pre-production Yak-3s for testing at the front. By war's end Pokryshev had been promoted to lieutenant colonel, having flown 309 sorties and fought 77 air combats. He scored 31 individual and seven shared victories, claiming roughly half of his kills while flying various models of Yak fighter.

Serving alongside Pokryshev in 29 GIAP in late 1942 was fellow ace Andrei Vasil'evich Chirkov. He too had flown in the Winter War with Finland, where he was shot down by ground fire. In another coincidence, Chirkov had also been serving as a lieutenant with 158 IAP when Germany invaded. On 23 June 1941 he shot down a He 111 over Leningrad, but contrary to some accounts, he was flying an I-16 rather than a Yak-1. By the end of August he had scored seven victories, but had been wounded twice and shot down once.

Another 29 GIAP Yak-7B, although this aircraft displays a well-worn winter camouflage finish. Although the pilot of this particular aircraft remains unknown, ace Andrei Chirkov flew a similarly-finished Yak-7B – numbered 64 – with the unit at around this time (spring 1943) (*G F Petrov*)

Together with Pokryshev and several other pilots, Chirkov was transferred to 154 IAP in the autumn of 1941, and he spent 1942 flying the P-40. In January 1943 the regiment – now redesignated 29 GIAP – converted to the Yak-7.

On 4 February 1944 Maj Chirkov became an HSU, and shortly afterwards he was sent to command P-39-equipped 196 IAP. While flying the Airacobra, he had the dubious distinction of being shot down by 75-kill Finnish ace Hans Wind on 19 June, although he was able to return to Soviet lines. By the end of the war, Chirkov had survived 420 sorties and 78 air combats, scoring 29 individual and nine shared victories. About half of these were claimed with the Yak-7.

The Yak-1 was also an early participant in the air battles in the south, where one of its most interesting pilots was Boris Eryomin. He had joined the Soviet Air Force in 1930, and first saw combat at Lake Khasan in 1938 when serving as a flight mechanic/rear gunner in a TB-3 during the conflict with the Japanese. In his spare time, Eryomin had been receiving unofficial flight lessons in one of the unit's light aircraft. By late 1939 he had learned to handle the controls sufficiently well enough to be admitted to flying school. Upon graduation Eryomin was assigned to a reserve unit, from which several combat regiments were hastily formed following the German invasion. Initially, Eryomin's 296 IAP – which became 73 GIAP on 3 May 1943 – was equipped with the I-16.

It was while flying this type that he scored his first victory in late June 1941. In mid-July he was shot down by 'friendly' anti-aircraft fire and spent a month in hospital. After release, Eryomin rejoined 296 IAP, but the unit suffered such a severe attrition rate that by the end of September it had almost no airworthy aircraft. The regiment was withdrawn to re-equip with the Yak-1, and as one of the few suriving pilots with combat experience, Eryomin was designated commander of the 2nd Squadron. But Yaks were then in short supply, and the unit was prevented from returning to the front until early 1942.

Some of the first missions undertaken by Eryomin's Yak-equipped regiment saw it escorting bombers, although the bulk of the sorties flown by 296 IAP that first winter were against ground targets. Pilots used the fighter's guns and RS-82 rockets in a forlorn attempt to halt the German invasion. It was dangerous work, but it had to be done by Yak-1 regiments due to a chronic shortage of more capable Il-2s.

At first 296 IAP flew Yak-1s equipped with skis instead of wheels. Eryomin reported that these aircraft were very unsatisfactory because the extra weight and drag of the skis made the fighter slower. The skis themselves were also plagued by a variety of maintenance problems. If one happened to fall out of its well during flight, either because of combat damage, a failure of the retraction system or even a violent manoeuvre, the aircraft would be rendered uncontrollable.

**Boris Ivanovich Kovzan's early career is shrouded in uncertainty and contradictory legend. But he did receive the HSU, and ended the war with 28 victories to his name, including four scored by ramming attacks. The bulk of of these kills were scored flying Yaks with 744 IAP (*RART*)**

**During the winter of 1942-43 a major campaign was run to collect money for donation aircraft. The populace of the Saratov region appear to have been very generous, and the end result of their donations is seen here – a delegation of local officials present their region's Yak-1B to the VVS. The inscription on the fighter's fuselage can only partially be discerned, but it seems to indicate that the aircraft was donated by the workers employed by Saratov's Karl Marx Film Theatre (*G F Petrov*)**

Pilots also had to exercise greater care when landing, since the angle of approach was much less forgiving than with wheels. Even then, the skis proved particularly vulnerable, and were in continuous need of repair. Yet, it was while flying one of these machines that Eryomin scored one of his most famous victories.

An unidentified fighter pilot strikes a defiant pose in a donation Yak-1 identified as *Balashov collective farmer*, again from the Saratov region (*G F Petrov*)

The morning of 9 March 1942 was still thick with frost when Eryomin led his squadron of seven Yak-1s out to relieve the 1st Squadron on patrol over Soviet troops. Near the frontline, Eryomin spotted six Bf 109s at his altitude off to the right. A little below them was another formation of seven Ju 88s, followed by a third group of 12 Bf 109Es carrying bombs.

Seeking the element of surprise, Eryomin turned his formation away to the south-west and flew off, climbing for altitude. Then he turned back to the right and led his pilots in a diving attack. In the first pass two Ju 88s and two Bf 109s were downed. Then three more Bf 109s went down as they turned back for a second attack. As the Germans jettisoned their bombs and fled, Eryomin re-grouped his formation and broke off the combat. Two of his pilots, Skotnoi and Salomatin, had suffered damage to their aircraft, but they were able to remain in the fight to the end. None of the Soviet pilots was hurt in a battle which had yielded seven victories for no losses. Eryomin's personal score was two Bf 109s shot down. On the way home Eryomin's pilots flew a tight 'parade' formation, rather than the usual open combat spread.

Word of their success – dubbed the battle of 'seven versus 25' – swept the front, and then the entire nation, as military commanders and Soviet newspapers alike made the most of the victory. All the pilots were decorated, and duly received fan mail from across the USSR. Eryomin remembers this as being the very first time, to his knowledge, that Soviet fighters had inflicted such losses on an appreciably larger formation. Indeed, it was to be one of few Soviet successes in the air in 1942.

By mid May the Germans had turned the Soviet Kharkov attack into a disaster, encircling almost a million men. While Eryomin and many of the surviving pilots managed to escape in their Yaks, most of the unit's groundcrews were not so lucky. The remnants of 296 IAP were once again sent to the rear to re-group. The desperate situation at the front meant that they had little time for training, and as early as 30 May the regiment returned to the front to defend Kupyansk railway junction.

That first day, this key target was attacked by bombers, and Eryomin's flight was scrambled to intercept. Selecting a He 111, he closed in and aimed his first shots at the gunner in the dorsal turret, who quickly disappeared, his gun pointing uselessly upwards at the sky. Now that the gunner was seemingly out of action, Eryomin closed in to finish off the Heinkel. Suddenly, a burst of fire hit the nose of his aircraft, disabling the coolant system. The cockpit filled with white steam and the front of the cowling flew up, blocking the pilot's forward view. The He 111 gunner had been playing dead, waiting for the Soviet fighter to get in closer. Eryomin made a forced landing, while his wingmen finished off the Heinkel.

An entire series of Yak-1B donation aircraft were expressly dedicated *To the defenders of the Stalingrad Front*. This delegation presents a fighter *From the collective farmers of the named for Voroshilov collective farm, of Balakovskii District, Saratov Region* (G F Petrov)

By the end of July, 296 IAP was fighting on the outskirts of Stalingrad. The unit flew numerous missions on a daily basis, but Luftwaffe superiority both in terms of men and equipment made victories rare. The regiment frequently abandoned airfields throughout the summer.

On 24 August 296 IAP was visited by 8 Air Army CO Gen Khryukin. After a brief discussion with the regiment's CO, he summoned Eryomin and explained that they badly needed intelligence on the precise location of the German armoured spearhead. With his wingman, Karetin, he was ordered to fly a reconnaissance mission to Vertyachii Khutor. They would have an escort of six other Yaks. Khryukin ended with the chilling admonition, 'One of you must return!' They crossed the Volga at 19,500 ft, but shortly afterwards were spotted by a flight of six Bf 109s. They quickly attacked, being joined by four more German fighters. Alhough Eryomin knew his mission was to avoid combat, he was forced onto the offensive when he saw a Bf 109 latch onto the tail of an escorting Yak. Wheeling around, he fired a burst which drove the German off, saving his comrade. But now a serious dogfight was breaking out.

At the first opportunity, Eryomin and Karetin broke away in a steep dive to ground level. Evading the enemy, they were so low they even flew under telegraph wires. Fired at repeatedly by German troops, the Yak pilots were too low for ground fire to track them successfully. Eventually, they encountered the leading German tanks, marked their location and hurried back to Soviet territory. Both pilots landed

This Yak-1B displays the inscription *To the defenders of the Stalingrad Front from the farmers of the Bolshevik Collective Farm, Khvalynsk District, Saratov Region* (G F Petrov)

This unidentified pilot seems to be returning from a mission in the Yak-1B *To the defenders of the Stalingrad Front for the collective farmers of the Lysogor district, Saratov Region* (*G F Petrov*)

at the first available airfield with their fuel almost exhausted. Eryomin immediately telephoned his report to Khryukin, who thanked him for it.

In mid-September one of the neighbouring regiments was withdrawn to rebuild, passing its remaining Yak-7s to 296 IAP. Eryomin was amongst the handful of pilots to receive one, and he thought there were few differences between the new Yak and his familiar Yak-1. Indeed, he preferred the earlier fighter. However, the Yak-7 did have a radio, boasting both a transmitter and a receiver, and Eryomin recognised that this was a great advantage in combat.

On 20 September he was shot down while flying with an inexperienced wingman. He baled out and landed with wounds to his face, arm and leg. After brief hospitalisation, Eryomin returned to 296 IAP to complete his recovery.

In early October Gen Khryukin decided to form 9 GIAP, led by Lev Shestakov (15 and 11 shared kills) into an elite striking force, containing the best pilots from all the fighter regiments of the Air Army. Khryukin personally slected Eryomin to be a part of the unit, and he duly reported for duty still walking with a stick. Seeing the latter, Shestakov had only three words, 'Healing? You fly?' Eryomin assured him on both counts, and was given command of the 2nd Squadron. But

Boris Eryomin's Yak-1 was paid for by Ferapont Petrovich Golovatyi, and it is seen here soon after arriving in the frontline in December 1942. Eryomin was a member of 31 GIAP at the time (*G F Petrov*)

Boris Eryomin climbs from his donation Yak-1 in early 1943 (*G F Petrov*)

before returning to combat, Eryomin was transferred to 31 GIAP as its CO to replace the unit's commander, who had just been killed.

This unit had been selected as 8 Air Army's tactical reconnaissance regiment. Its pilots flew mainly in pairs, occasionally in fours, and very rarely in greater numbers, although they also flew regular fighter missions. They also had less occasion for scoring victories. Combat was permitted only when necessary to enable them to return with vital information. When Eryomin arrived, he found the regiment's morale shaken and its pilots disorganised. Each man flew and fought according to his own ideas, which obviously impaired discipline.

Eryomin received valuable reinforcements in the form of a group of experienced pilots from a recently-disbanded regiment, several of whom were destined to be made HSUs. On 1 December, in addition to other duties, Eryomin was also ordered to help with the interdiction of Luftwaffe transport aircraft that were attempting to supply Stalingrad.

Later that month Eryomin received a disturbing order from Gen Khryukin – fly back to Saratov to pick up a fighter. This instruction came in the middle of the great Soviet offensive, when every pilot and commander was needed at the front. To make matters worse, he was still new to his regiment. None of this mattered to Khryukin, as this was a special presentation aircraft. As the intended recipient, Eryomin had to attend the ceremony. The Yak had been donated by Ferapont Petrovich Golovatyi, and it was one of two fighters donated during the war by this collective farmer from the Saratov region. He had specified that his gift should go to the Stalingrad Front, and Eryomin was chosen to receive it

After the snow melted in the spring of 1943, Eryomin's fighter was repainted in standard summer camouflage, after which the donation inscription was carefully reapplied. By the summer of 1944 this long-lived aircraft had exceeded its permitted flying hours, and when Eryomin received a new one, it was put on display in Saratov – where this photograph was taken post-war (*G F Petrov*)

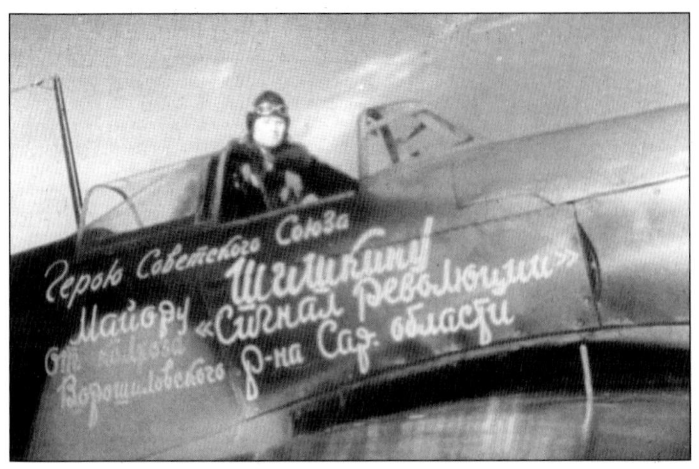


This Yak-1B was also donated in the winter of 1942, and it too is seen here in a new finish the following spring. The fighter was specially donated *To Hero of the Soviet Union, Maj Shishkin from the Signal of the Revolution Collective Farm, Voroshilovsk District, Saratov Region*. Vasilii Ivanovich Shishkin commanded 55 GIAP and scored 15 individual and 16 shared victories. The spinners of all the donated fighters in his regiment were painted red (*G F Petrov*)

because of his combat successes, and his fame in the well-publicised 'Seven against 25 battle' on 9 March. In addition, he came from the same district as the donor.

In January 1943 Eryomin's regiment flew intensified reconnaissance missions over German forces beyond Stalingrad. It also provided the fighter escort for Il-2s and Pe-2s, resulting in more air combat and increased opportunities for victories. In mid February, Eryomin shot down a Ju 87 over Manych, noting that it was the third kill he had scored with Golovatyi's Yak. Later in the month he downed a Ju 88 south of Bataisk.

From March, 31 GIAP supported offensives launched at the Mius River and near Taganrog, on the north coast of the Sea of Azov. It then helped in the fight to liberate southern Ukraine and the Donbass region.

In late December 1943 Eryomin was called to headquarters by Gen Sidnev and appointed Deputy CO of 6 GIAD – a job which took him away from his regiment, although he could still fly regularly.

Sidnev was made CO of 13 IAK (Fighter Air Corps) in February 1944 and his place taken by Col Iosif Geibo. Eryomin and Geibo did not get on, and this was one of the main reasons why the veteran ace did not receive the HSU during the war.

On 25 May 1944, Eryomin read in *Pravda* that Ferapont Petrovich Golovatyi was to present the VVS (Army Air Forces) with a second Yak gift. The story added that he had 'asked that the aircraft be presented to Maj Eryomin'. Eryomin was flown back to Saratov in a courier aircraft to participate in the 29 May handing over ceremony, which saw him receive an early Yak-3 from the very first production batch months before the type began to reach the front in quantity. Eryomin made a special plea at the time for a second Yak-3 to be assigned to his division so that his wingman might have a comparable aircraft. As a result, his friend (and 31 GIAP Deputy CO) Maj Sergei Evtikhov also received an early Yak-3.

Although Eryomin continued to fly combat sorties whenever possible, his command duties usually kept him on the ground. When he could not fly the Yak himself, he let leading pilots from the division borrow it.

The first real opportunity to use the Yak-3s in combat came in July during the L'vov-Sandomir operation, and an early encounter with the enemy in August had potentially disastrous ramifications.

The Germans were attempting to disrupt the Vistula river crossing, with numerous bomber formations attempting to penetrate Soviet air cover. When one group managed to approach the bridgehead late one evening, they were attacked by Soviet fighters and prevented from bombing accurately. A stick of bombs came very close to one of the bridges, however, tearing several boats loose. There was no serious damage or injury, and the bridgehead continued to function. But the local commander was panicked by the attack, and he sent an alarmist

Eryomin's second gift from Golovatyi was this Yak-3, received in late May 1944. The inscription reads *From Ferapont Petrovich Golovatyi. 2nd aircraft for the final destruction of the enemy* (*V Kulikov*)

report that the bridgehead had been knocked out. The communique eventually made it to 2 Ukrainian Front HQ, which then blamed the fighter pilots for allowing the bridge to be bombed without interference.

The Front Commander was Marshal Konev, an officer notorious for his temper. He demanded that the pilots responsible (from 6 GIAD regiments) be hauled before a tribunal. They would normally have stood little chance with the Front Commander baying for a sacrifice, but Eryomin was offended by the whole affair. He knew the bridgehead had not been touched, so he and Chief-of-Staff Suyakov defended the accused pilots. Confirming that the bridgehead had suffered no significant damage, Suyakov flew to Air Army headquarters to plead the case. Luckily, Marshal Novikov happened to be making a tour of inspection, which enabled Suyakov to put the pilots' case directly to the VVS Commander-in-Chief. Soon afterwards, the Representative of the Front Staff arrived at the bridgehead and came to the conclusion that the pilots were blameless of an offence which had not been committed.

At the end of August 1944, 6 GIAD was transferred to 2 Ukrainian Front to reinforce the offensive into Rumania and Hungary. Eryomin ended the war in Czechoslovakia, claiming his last kill (a Fw 190) on 10 May 1945. He had flown 342 sorties, including 100 ground attack and 102 reconnaissance missions, and was credited with eight individual and 15 shared victories in more than 60 air combats. Boris Eryomin continued his distinguished career in the air force post-war, and received his HSU in 1990.

Three of the other pilots who participated in the 'seven against 25' battle remained with 296 IAP after Eryomin was posted away and eventually became aces. Capt Ivan

Eryomin climbs into the cockpit of his Yak-3. The *2 c-t* inscription ahead of the victory stars signifies *2 Samolyot* (his second aircraft) (*RART*)

Ivanovich Zapryagaev had flown with the regiment from the start of the war, and by the time of the celebrated battle, he was Eryomin's deputy. Made squadron CO after the latter's transfer, Zapryagaev duly became commander of the redesignated 73 GIAP in July 1943. In September 1944 he was promoted to other duties, but was killed in 1945 after scoring 11 victories.

**Aleksei Reshetov flew this Yak-1 during 1942. Its inscription reads *Shmert Fashchisty*, which seems to be a grammatical mistake because it should read *Shmert Fashchistam* ('Death to the Fascists') (*RART*)**

Aleksandr Vasil'evich Martynov had also flown with 296 IAP from the start of the war, and he scored his first victory (a Bf 109) on 8 March 1942. The following day he shot down one of the Ju 88s destroyed in the 'seven against 25' battle. By August 1942 he had scored 17 individual and 16 shared victories, and was made an HSU. Martynov was among the 296 IAP pilots sent to 9 GIAP, but like Eryomin, his assignment was only brief, for he was sent back to 296 IAP. When future female aces Lilya Litvyak and Katerina Budanova were transferred to his unit in the autumn of 1942, Martynov often flew with the latter on his wing. It appears that Martynov scored only one more victory before being withdrawn from combat in 1943 and sent to the Advanced Navigation School.

Aleksei Frolovich Salomatin was serving as an instructor when the Germans invaded, and he was sent to 296 IAP in July 1941. During the battle of 'seven against 25' he shot down a Bf 109, and by the autumn he was a senior lieutenant. When Litvyak and Budanova arrived, he played an influential role in persuading the regiment commander to permit them to stay and prove themselves, volunteering to have one fly on his wing. Lilya Litvyak soon became his fiancee, and he flew combat missions with her photograph in his cockpit. On 1 May 1943, having flown 266 sorties and become a HSU, Salomatin was promoted to captain. Three weeks later he was killed while testing an aircraft that had just returned from maintenance, the Yak spinning in directly over the airfield. At the time of his death Salomatin had scored 17 individual and 22 shared kills.

Aleksei Mikhailovich Reshetov was another early Yak-1 ace, having completed his flying training in 1940. On 22 June 1941 he scored his first victory at 0430 hrs while flying a Polikarpov fighter with 239 IAP. Two months later he was reassigned to 273 IAP (31 GIAP from 21 November 1942), which was being reformed with LaGG-3s after having been all but annihilated during the first weeks of the war. In early 1942 the regiment received Yak-1s.

**Capt Nikolai Elizarovich Glazov initially flew with 11 IAP, but transferred to 31 IAP in 1942 and received the HSU on 1 May 1943. He had scored 17 individual and seven shared victories by the time he was killed while ramming a Fw 189 on 30 July 1943 *(G F Petrov)***

By February 1943 Reshetov had been promoted to captain and given command of the 1st Squadron. By then he had flown 432 sorties, survived 100 combats had 11 individual

**Above and right**
**In these two photographs, M D Baranov taxies out at the start of a sortie in his Yak-1 on the South-western Front in the summer of 1942. Note his 23 victory stars behind the cockpit, and the inscription *Groza fashchistov M. D. Baranov*, ('Terror of the fascists, M. D. Baranov') (*V Kulikov*)**

**Now returned from the mission, the Yak-1 is tended to by Baranov's groundcrew, one of whom applies a 24th star to the scoreboard. While all this is going on behind him, Baranov (centre) himself speaks to his ground staff (*V Kulikov*)**

**A close up photograph of the latest addition to the scoreboard (*V Kulikov*)**

and eight shared victories. He received the HSU on 1 May and was promoted to major.

Although the unit had by now become 31 GIAP, it continued to fly the elderly Yak-1B during 1943-44 because its pilots enjoyed the fighter's superior manoeuvrability. In the autumn of the 1943 Reshetov received a special dedication aircraft, and in August 1944 the Yak-3s finally arrived. On one occasion in 1945, he led six Yak-3s against 48 Fw 190s over Esztergom, destroying eight for no loss. By war's end Reshetov had been promoted to major, flown 821 sorties, of which more than 250 were reconnaissance missions, fought 200 air combats and scored 36 individual and eight shared victories.

Another famous early Yak ace was Mikhail Dmitrievich Baranov, who also graduated from flying school in 1940. In June 1941 he became a flight commander with 183 IAP, which was in the process of forming in the Odessa Military District when the Germans invaded. Having no aircraft, the regiment withdrew to the Volga, where it received MiG-3s and Yak-1s, before returning to the front in mid September.

Baranov was lucky enough to fly the Yak-1 right from the start, and on 22 September he destroyed a Bf 109 and a Hs 126 artillery spotting aircraft. A few days later it was his turn to be shot down, taking to his parachute after being wounded in the leg. Baranov landed behind enemy lines, and he spent the next two weeks evading capture (he even shot a German soldier) until he could escape into friendly territory.

On 8 November Baranov was returning from a ground-strafing mission when he saw another Hs 126. Gaining altitude, he then dived at the Henschel and shot it down before escorting fighters were alerted to his presence. As he recovered from his attack, Baranov spotted a flight of four Bf 109s nearby. Feeling it was his lucky day, he decided to take a chance. If he could take them by surprise, he might be able to steal up on one,

**A posed photograph of Baranov in his Yak-1 receiving congratulations following yet another successful sortie *(G F Petrov)***

shoot it down and dive away before the others could react. But he was not able to escape so easily. After shooting down the first Bf 109, Baranov's Yak was damaged before he could break off and return home.

By June 1942 he had completed 176 sorties, shooting down 24 enemy aircraft, and destroying another six on the ground.

On 6 August, while escorting Il-2s over Kotel'nikovo, Baranov led his section of four Yaks in an attack on a formation of 25 Bf 109s and Ju 87s. He attacked and shot down the fighter leader, and then found a second on his tail. Turning inside and diving away, Baranov found himself near the Stukas, one of which he shot down. On the return flight, he spotted a flight of Bf 109s stalking the Ilyushins. Baranov attacked, shooting down one of the German fighters before running out of ammunition. He then achieved his fourth kill of the mission by ramming a second fighter, after which he parachuted to safety. Baranov was awarded the HSU on 12 August, and promoted to captain, following this mission.

**This Yak-1 is sometimes associated with 183 IAP ace M D Baranov, but apparently incorrectly. While the ten victory stars are in the same location as those carried on Baranov's fighter, this example has a radio mast, while the aircraft seen in the photographs on pages 29 and 30 clearly lacks one. The inscription reads *Smert za smert* ('Death for death'). The pilot of this particular machine remains unknown, but the figure seen here in the foreground with the map is Battalion Commissar V L Stelimashchuk (*G F Petrov*)**

In October 1942 he was made deputy CO of 9 GIAP, despite suffering continuing medical problems as a result of his August ramming attack. In mid November he almost crashed as a result of in-flight leg cramps, and he was sent to hospital for treatment and recuperation. Baranov did not return until 15 January 1943, and 48 hours later he attempted to demonstrate his return to combatworthiness by performing a series of aerobatic manoeuvres in a Yak-1. The aircraft soon fell into a spin, however, and exploded when it hit the ground, killing Baranov. His final score was 24 individual and 28 shared victories, achieved in 285 missions and 85 combats. He also destroyed six aircraft on the ground.

292 IAP's Deputy CO Anton Dmitrievich Yakimenko was already a HSU when the Germans invaded, having won the accolade for scoring three individual and four shared victories against the Japanese at Khalkin Gol in 1939. By November 1941 he had been appointed CO of 427 IAP (later 151 GIAP). As a commander, Yakimenko was respected for his concern for subordinates, and for taking care to assure that his pilots were all properly trained before going into combat.

Having been in the frontline since June 1941, Yakimenko was badly wounded in the head during the Jassy-Kishinev operation in the summer of 1944. Returning to his unit in the final weeks of that year, the ace was

Snr Lt V F Korobov flew this Yak-1 with 34 IAP and scored 18 victories (*G F Petrov*)

involved in a large-scale engagment on 21 November while leading eight Yak-9s that were protecting ground forces at Yasberen. He encountered 20 German fighters, Yakimenko attacking head-on and shooting down a Bf 109, while the remaining pilots in the flight scored a further four kills.

In late December he took over as CO of 150 GIAP (previously 183 IAP), and there remains some dispute about his combat record thereafter. Most sources agree that he flew 241 missions and scored 13 individual and 35 shared victories in 29 air combats, in addition to his Khalkin Gol kills. But another reliable source credits him with 38 individual victories, while a third puts his score at 31 individual and 35 shared victories between 1941-45. Yakimenko did not keep count of his own victories, or those of subordinates. 'Our job is scoring victories. Counting them is the enemy's job', he would say. Yakimenko survived to retire in 1972, having completed 7934 flights in 36 different types of aircraft ranging from the World War 1 era R-1 to the MiG-21 – from Mach 0.1 to Mach 2.2!

Yet another pilot who achieved fame flying the Yak-1 during the early stages of the war was Ivan Ivanovich Kleshchyov, whose success allowed him to become something of a celebrity and a playboy. Kleshchyov joined the Red Air Force in 1937, and scored his first victory over Khalkin Gol in 1939. By June 1941 he was already a major, and a squadron commander in 521 IAP, which was in the process of forming on the Western Front. Initially, the regiment operated the LaGG-3, and by March 1942 Kleshchyov had scored six individual and 13 shared victories, for which he received the HSU on 5 May that same year. In April he was appointed CO of 434

Surprisingly, very few photographs of the famous 434 IAP/32 GIAP have surfaced. This one shows a presentation Yak-7B in the winter of 1942-43. The dedication reads *K-Z Politotdelets to the defenders of Stalingrad, The Red Banner Political Section member to the Defenders of Stalingrad* (*G F Petrov*)

IAP, which was re-equipping with the Yak-1. Kleshchyov brought several other pilots with him, and under his command the regiment was to earn fame and eventually become 32 GIAP in November 1942.

Already a national hero by the time he became a regimental commander, Kleshchyov was hand-picked for the assignment by Vasilii Stalin. As another benefit of his status as a Soviet celebrity, Kleshchyov was living with the well-known Soviet film star Zoya Fyodorova.

After training for 12-14 hours a day for about a month, 434 IAP had been declared ready for combat and thrown into the fight on the South-western Front at Stalingrad on 13 June 1942. Kleshchyov led the first combat flight, which comprised ten Yaks providing air cover to the ground forces. When they were bounced by 15 Bf 109s coming out of the sun, he counter-attacked, and the clash ended with three kills – one scored by Kleshchyov himself – without any losses. There was another battle fought on the 15th, when 17 Yaks intercepted 28 Bf 109s. This time 434 IAP lost three fighters shot down, but it did claim four Bf 109s in return, including another to Kleshchyov.

The intense fighting continued, pilots often flying as many as five or six sorties a day. Within three weeks the regiment, which had begun with 21 fighters, had no aircraft left, and it was withdrawn to the Moscow region to reform. 434 IAP had flown about 800 missions and scored 35 kills.

This time the regiment received a large intake of experienced pilots, many of whom had been serving as instructors at the Kacha flight school. These pilots did not have any tactical experience, but they did have between 700 and 2000 hours of flight time each – quite an advantage over the average new pilot, who was being hurried to the front with between 10 and 20 hours in the cockpit.

Within a week the regiment (now increased to three squadrons) was able to return to the front. It had also received some Yak-7Bs. From 13 July 434 IAP was based at Gumrak, near Stalingrad, and it managed to complete 827 sorties and score 55 kills before using up its aircraft once

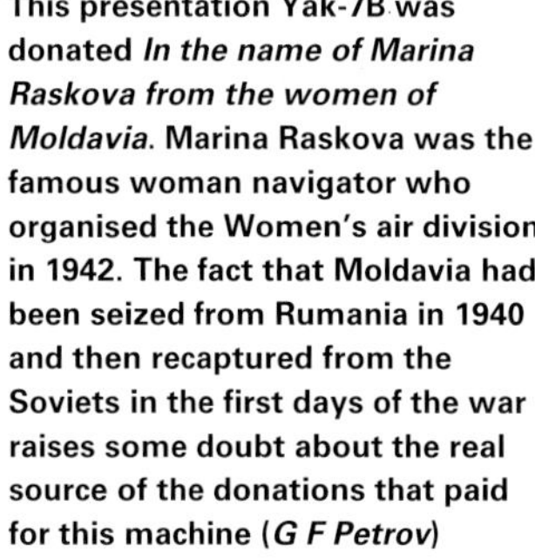

**This presentation Yak-7B was donated *In the name of Marina Raskova from the women of Moldavia*. Marina Raskova was the famous woman navigator who organised the Women's air division in 1942. The fact that Moldavia had been seized from Rumania in 1940 and then recaptured from the Soviets in the first days of the war raises some doubt about the real source of the donations that paid for this machine (*G F Petrov*)**

again in just three weeks. The single most notable day came on 26 July, thanks to particularly heavy Luftwaffe activity. Every pilot had to fly six or seven missions, with the unit fighting 11 air battles in total and claiming 34 kills. 434 IAP lost only three machines, one of whose pilots managed to bale out safely. On 3 August the regiment again stood down for replenishment.

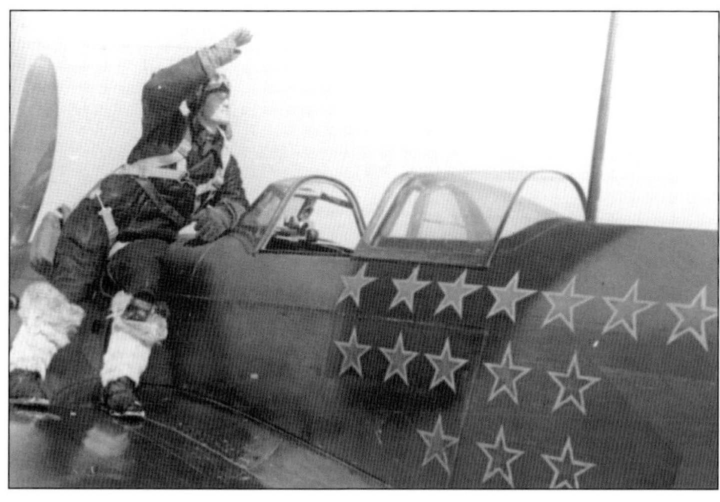

Capt Nikolai Aleksandrovich Kozlov of 788 IAP scans the sky from the wing of his Yak-1B in May 1943. He survived the war with 18 individual and five shared kills from 620 sorties (*G F Petrov*)

Now it was to be strengthened as an elite unit, being staffed by the best pilots that A F Semyonov of the Fighter Inspectorate and Kleshchyov could find, including Sergei Dolgushin. Among the new regiment members were two sons of Anastas Mikoyan and female fighter pilots detached from the women's 587 IAP.

The regiment returned to the Stalingrad front and flew its first mission on 16 September, the assault on the city having begun three days before. This intense period of operations saw pilots flying five or six missions a day, and by the end of the month the regiment was reduced to one-third strength in aircraft and 15 fewer pilots.

During his first mission back in action Kleshchyov shot down a Bf 109 and a Ju 87 over Kotluban, but on 19 September he was shot down in flames. Despite suffering from burns he managed to bale out, and had to spend time in hospital. A F Semyonov, serving with the unit in his capacity as a representative of the Fighter Inspectorate, took temporary charge of the regiment, which was again withdrawn on 3 October.

Since 15 June, 434 IAP had flown 2060 combat flights and shot down 173 aircraft. Although 'wiped out' three times, this is misleading, since it refers to aircraft lost, including those shot down in combat, destroyed on the ground, lost in accidents and damaged too seriously for field repairs. In November 434 IAP was honoured by becoming 32 GIAP.

**In the spring of 1942 an entire squadron of Yak-7As was bought with funds collected by the Komsomol (Young Communist League) and assigned to 12 GIAP. The inscription on the nearest aircraft reads *Novosibirskii Komsomol*, and Number 7 is *Komsomol Kuzbassa* (*G F Petrov*)**

**Left**
**Nikolai Kozlov assumes a more formal pose by his aircraft. Winner of the HSU, Kozlov also flew I-16s with 162 IAP, claiming at least four kills (one rammed) between June and September 1941. He then served briefly with 439 IAP, before joining 788 IAP. Promoted to captain during the fighting over Kuban River, Kozlov was transferred to 907 IAP at Kursk in the summer of 1943. He remained with the unit until war's end (*G F Petrov*)**

Kleshchyov was killed on 31 December 1942. He had wanted to fly back to Moscow to spend the new year with Zoya Fyodorova, and persisted in doing so despite the poor flying weather. As a gift, he brought with him two geese, obtained from a local farm, and put them in the open storage space behind the cockpit of his Yak. That evening, a local peasant came to 32 GIAP's airfield and reported that he had found the wreck of a fighter aircraft, in the cockpit of which had been the pilot and two geese.

Kleshchyov had flown 380 sorties, but his final victory score is disputed. Officially, it was 16 individual and 32 shared kills, although a recent historian credits him with 17 individual and 18 shared victories, while fellow 32 GIAP pilot Stepan Mikoyan puts the score at 24 and 32. The latter also suggested that had he not perished in an avoidable accident, Kleshchyov might have surpassed both Pokryshkin and Kozhedub by war's end. After Kleshchyov's death, Vasilii Stalin took over command of the regiment until May 1943.

One of the pilots Ivan Kleshchyov brought from 521 IAP to 434 IAP in April 1942 was Vladimir Yakovlevich Alkidov. He had been wounded on the first day of the war when his regiment was strafed at Tarnopol by Ju 88s. Following his release from hospital, he was sent to 521 IAP. There, he met Kleshchyov, who made him a flight commander with 434 IAP.

On 13 June 1942 Alkidov took part in an air battle against a superior number of Bf 109s, but nevertheless managed to shoot one down. He was, however, wounded both in his face and in the left side of his body. Alkidov kept flying nonetheless, and eventually managed to land at a forward airfield, from where he was rushed to hospital. By August he had flown 300 missions and scored ten kills, and he duly received the HSU on the 12th, together with promotion to captain. Shot up once again just weeks later and forced to bale out with leg and arm wounds, Alkidov was captured. Somehow, he managed to escape and return to his own lines. Sent back to hospital, Alkidov did not return to flying status.

Another arrival from 521 IAP was Nikolai Aleksandrovich Karnachyonok, who had been in combat from the start of the war. By July 1942 Lt Karnachyonok had flown 349 sorties and shot down ten aircraft, to which score he added a Ju 87 on 17 September. Five days later he was killed near Kotluban after shooting down a bomber to raise his total to 12 victories – Karnachyonok and his wingman collided after downing a Bf 109, their wrecked aircraft almost falling on top of their last victim. Karnachyonok was made a posthumous HSU on 23 November, having scored at least 12 and one shared victories.

Vasilii Petrovich Babkov graduated from flying school in 1937 and began the war with I-16-equipped 123 IAP in the Brest area. He too was soon posted to 521 IAP, where he became friendly with Ivan Kleshchyov, who took him to 434 IAP in April 1942 and made him regimental navigator and later deputy CO for flight crews. Babkov was promoted to major in August, by which time he had completed 287 sorties and shot down 11 aircraft individually and shared in the destruction of nine others during 68 air battles. In September Babkov was allocated a Yak-7B, and he used it to claim a victory on the 6th, followed by two Ju 88s on the 20th. He was made a HSU on 23 November.

From January 1943 Babkov served as Vasilii Stalin's deputy regimental CO, and in May he was transferred out at the same time as Stalin and Dolgushin. This may have been a part of the general shake-up resulting from Stalin's poor leadership, but Babkov was not harmed by it for he was sent to command the Lavochkin-equipped 88 GIAP. Just prior to war's end he became CO of 5 GIAD, and by VE-Day he had flown 465 sorties and scored 23 individual and 11 shared victories in 100 air combats. Two-thirds of his victories had probably been scored in Yaks. He was also shot down four times.

Babkov remained in the service until 1986, retiring as a colonel general. He continued flying almost until the end of his military career, and was still flying supersonic jets beyond the age of 60. Indeed, he flew almost every fighter in service with the Soviet Air Forces.

Perhaps the best of the pilots accompanying Kleshchyov from 521 IAP was Andrei Yakovlevich Baklan. He had graduated from flying school in 1938 and seen combat in the I-153 with the 434th IAP during the 1939 Winter War with Finland. In June 1941 his regiment was destroyed within days, and it reformed with Yak-1s. In July Baklan claimed his first victory when he shot down a Bf 109 over Novgorod-Severskii. By February 1942 he had claimed his six kills (three Bf 109s, two Ju 88 and one Hs 126), earning him a transfer to 521 IAP and assignment to Ivan Kleshchyov's squadron.

In March Baklan's flight intercepted a large formation of Ju 87s, escorted by Bf 109s. In the ensuing dogfight he downed a Ju 87 and a fighter, but during the battle he

(*text continues on page 47*)

**In addition to the Komsomol, the Young Pioneers (a communist organisation for young children) also purchased aircraft. This Yak-7 was christened the *Novosibirskii Pioner* (*V Kulikov*)**

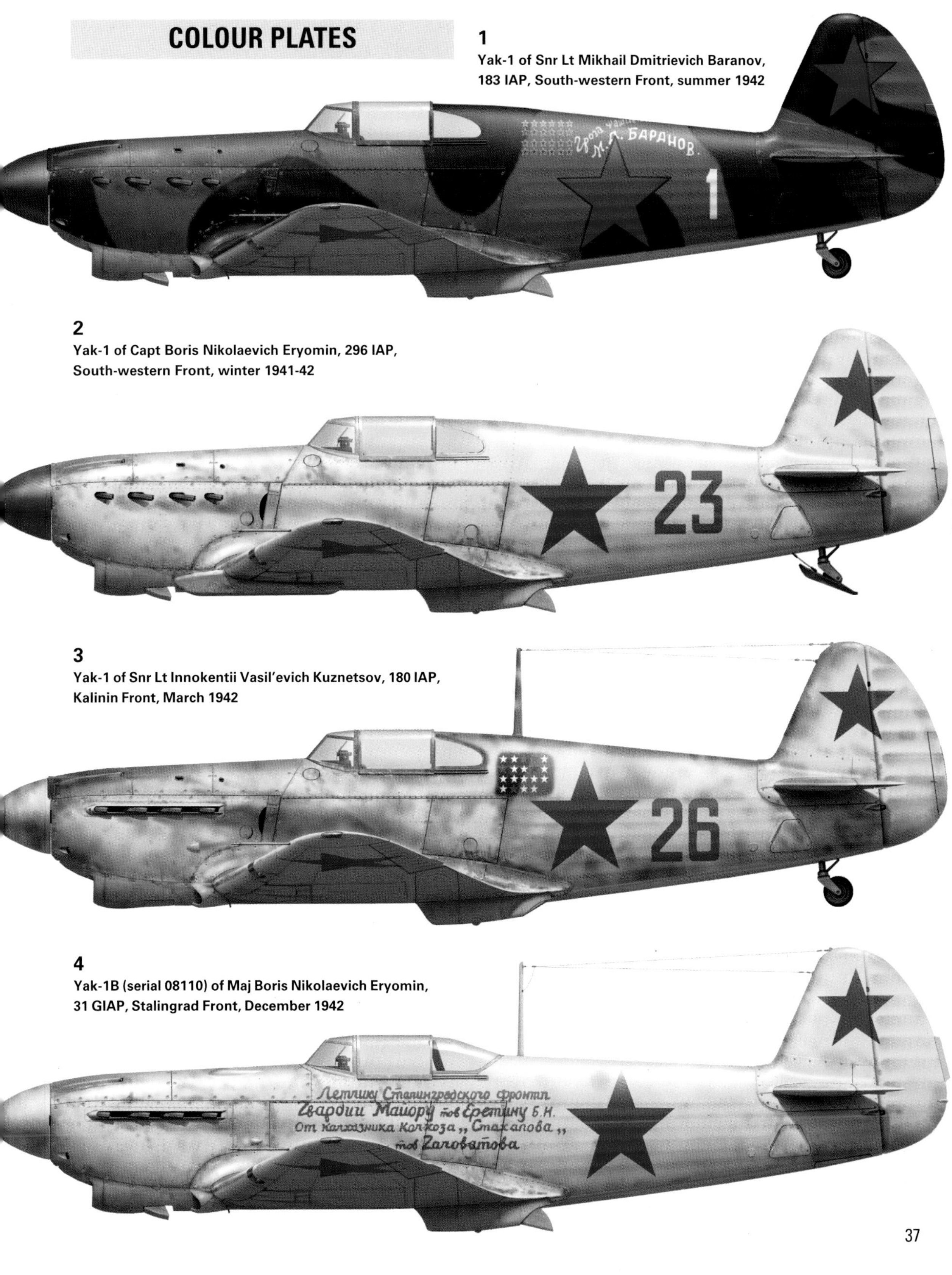


## COLOUR PLATES

**1**
**Yak-1 of Snr Lt Mikhail Dmitrievich Baranov, 183 IAP, South-western Front, summer 1942**

**2**
**Yak-1 of Capt Boris Nikolaevich Eryomin, 296 IAP, South-western Front, winter 1941-42**

**3**
**Yak-1 of Snr Lt Innokentii Vasil'evich Kuznetsov, 180 IAP, Kalinin Front, March 1942**

**4**
**Yak-1B (serial 08110) of Maj Boris Nikolaevich Eryomin, 31 GIAP, Stalingrad Front, December 1942**

**5**
Yak-1B (serial 08110) of Maj Boris Nikolaevich Eryomin, 31 GIAP, Stalingrad Front, summer 1943

**6**
Yak-1B of Maj Aleksei Mikhailovich Reshetov, 31 GIAP, 4 Ukrainian Front, autumn 1943

**7**
Yak-1B of Lt Lilya Vladimirovna Litvyak, 296 IAP, South Front, summer 1943

**8**
Yak-1B of Capt Nikolai Aleksandrovich Kozlov, 910 IAP (PVO unit), Borisoglebsk, February 1943

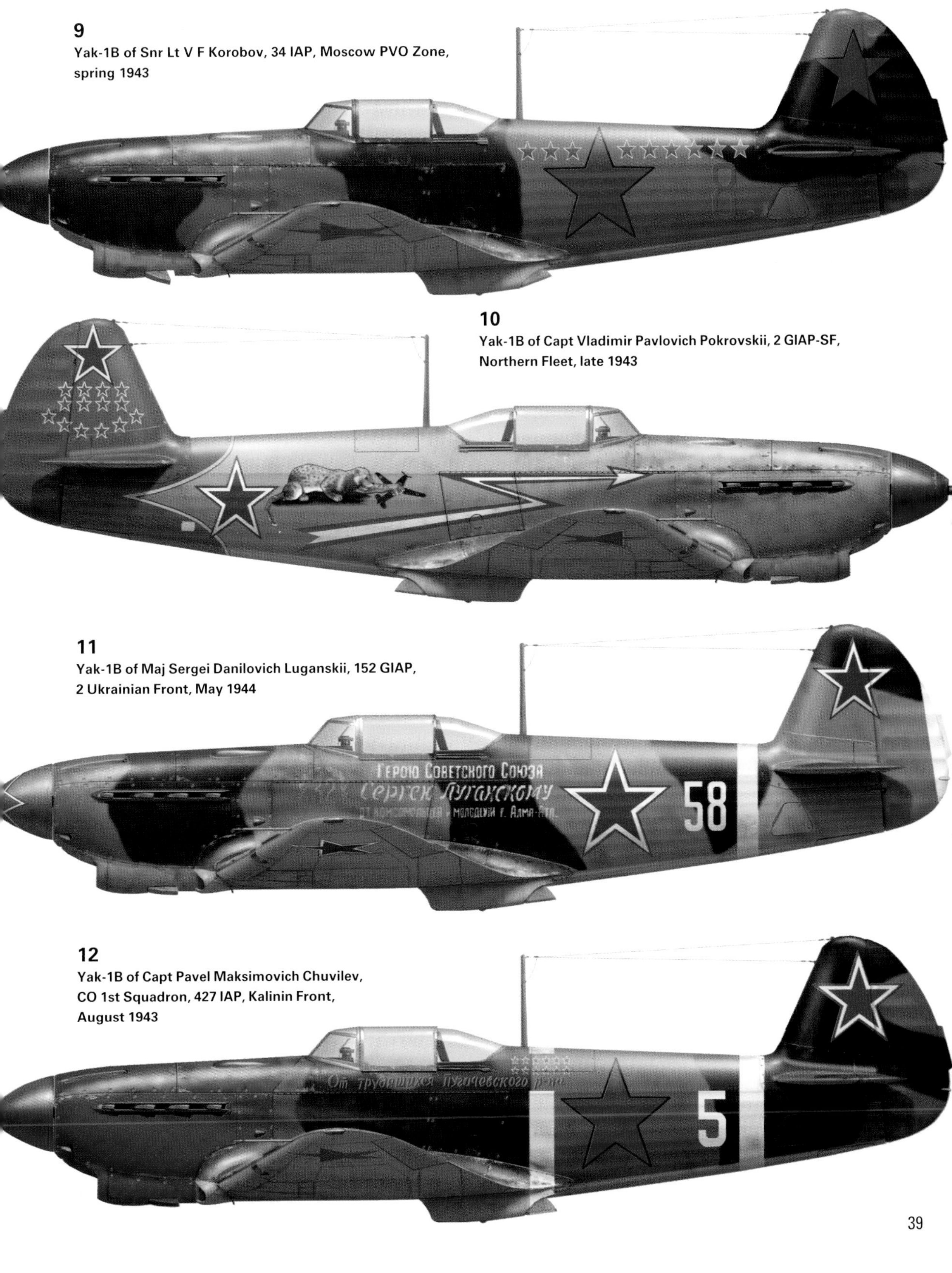


**9**
Yak-1B of Snr Lt V F Korobov, 34 IAP, Moscow PVO Zone, spring 1943

**10**
Yak-1B of Capt Vladimir Pavlovich Pokrovskii, 2 GIAP-SF, Northern Fleet, late 1943

**11**
Yak-1B of Maj Sergei Danilovich Luganskii, 152 GIAP, 2 Ukrainian Front, May 1944

**12**
Yak-1B of Capt Pavel Maksimovich Chuvilev, CO 1st Squadron, 427 IAP, Kalinin Front, August 1943

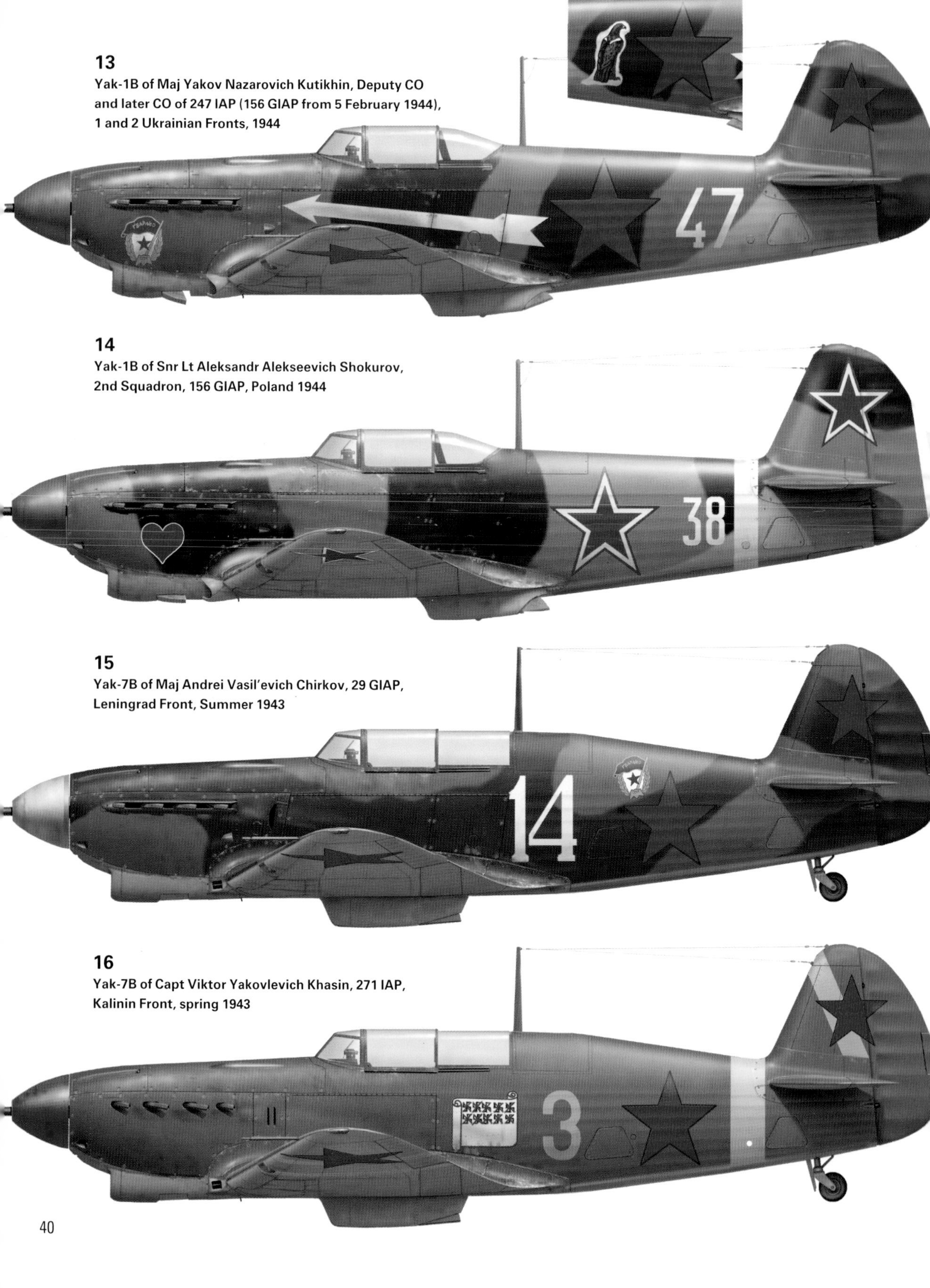


**13**
Yak-1B of Maj Yakov Nazarovich Kutikhin, Deputy CO and later CO of 247 IAP (156 GIAP from 5 February 1944), 1 and 2 Ukrainian Fronts, 1944

**14**
Yak-1B of Snr Lt Aleksandr Alekseevich Shokurov, 2nd Squadron, 156 GIAP, Poland 1944

**15**
Yak-7B of Maj Andrei Vasil'evich Chirkov, 29 GIAP, Leningrad Front, Summer 1943

**16**
Yak-7B of Capt Viktor Yakovlevich Khasin, 271 IAP, Kalinin Front, spring 1943

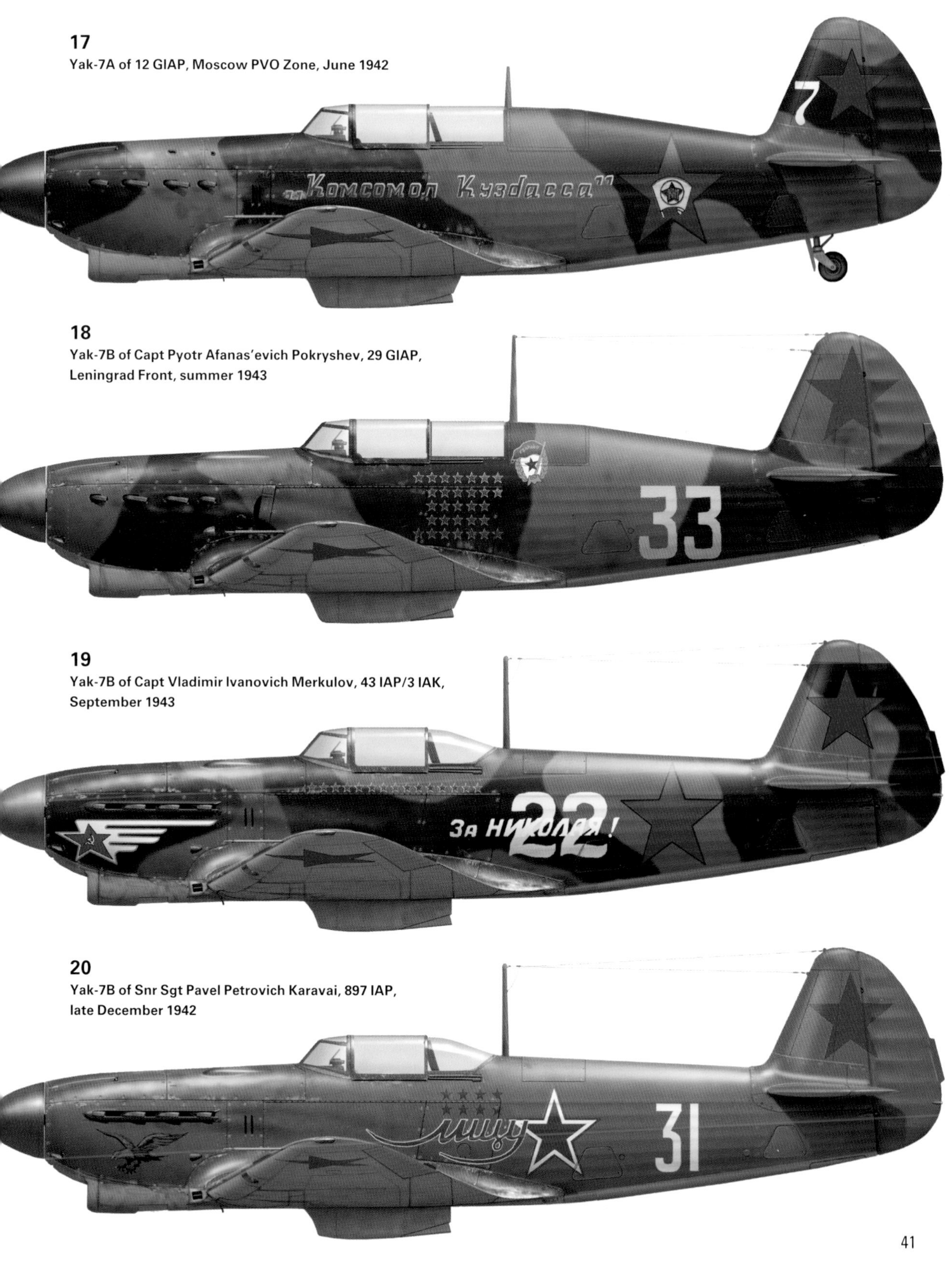


**17**
**Yak-7A of 12 GIAP, Moscow PVO Zone, June 1942**

**18**
**Yak-7B of Capt Pyotr Afanas'evich Pokryshev, 29 GIAP, Leningrad Front, summer 1943**

**19**
**Yak-7B of Capt Vladimir Ivanovich Merkulov, 43 IAP/3 IAK, September 1943**

**20**
**Yak-7B of Snr Sgt Pavel Petrovich Karavai, 897 IAP, late December 1942**

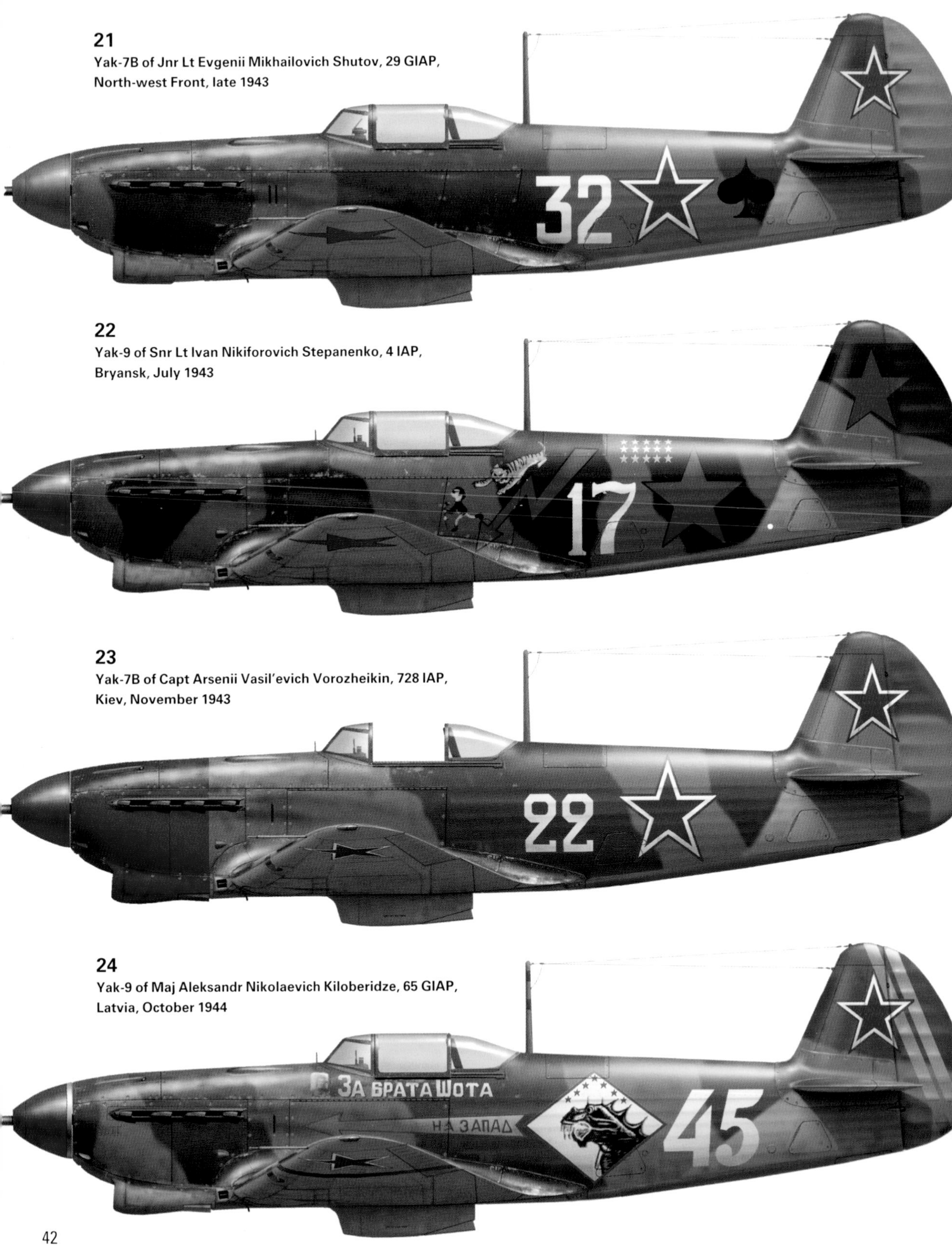


**21**
Yak-7B of Jnr Lt Evgenii Mikhailovich Shutov, 29 GIAP, North-west Front, late 1943

**22**
Yak-9 of Snr Lt Ivan Nikiforovich Stepanenko, 4 IAP, Bryansk, July 1943

**23**
Yak-7B of Capt Arsenii Vasil'evich Vorozheikin, 728 IAP, Kiev, November 1943

**24**
Yak-9 of Maj Aleksandr Nikolaevich Kiloberidze, 65 GIAP, Latvia, October 1944

**25**
Yak-9 of Capt Nikolai Fyodorovich Denchik, 64 GIAP, Belorussia, early 1944

**26**
Yak-9 of Maj Abrek Arkad'evich Barsht, 118 OKRAP (*Otdel'nyi Korrektirovochnyi Razvedyvatel'nyi Aviatsionnyi Polk* - Separate Artillery Reconnaissance Air Regiment), 1 Ukrainian Front, late 1944

**27**
Yak-9D of Snr Lt Mikhail Ivanovich Grib, 6 GIAP-ChF, Crimea, May 1944

**28**
Yak-9D of Lt Col Mikhail Vasil'evich Avdeev, 6 GIAP-ChF, Crimea, May 1944

**29**
Yak-9T of Maj Ivan Nikiforovich Stepanenko, 4 IAP,
2 Baltic Front, December 1944

**30**
Yak-9T of Snr Lt Aleksandr Ivanovich Vybornov, 728 IAP,
2 Ukrainian Front, autumn 1944

**31**
Yak-9T of Snr Lt Dmitrii Dmitrievich Tormakhov, 267 IAP,
Rumania, June 1944

**32**
Yak-9T of Capt Ivan Ivanovich Vetrov, 66 GIAP,
1 Baltic Front, early June 1944

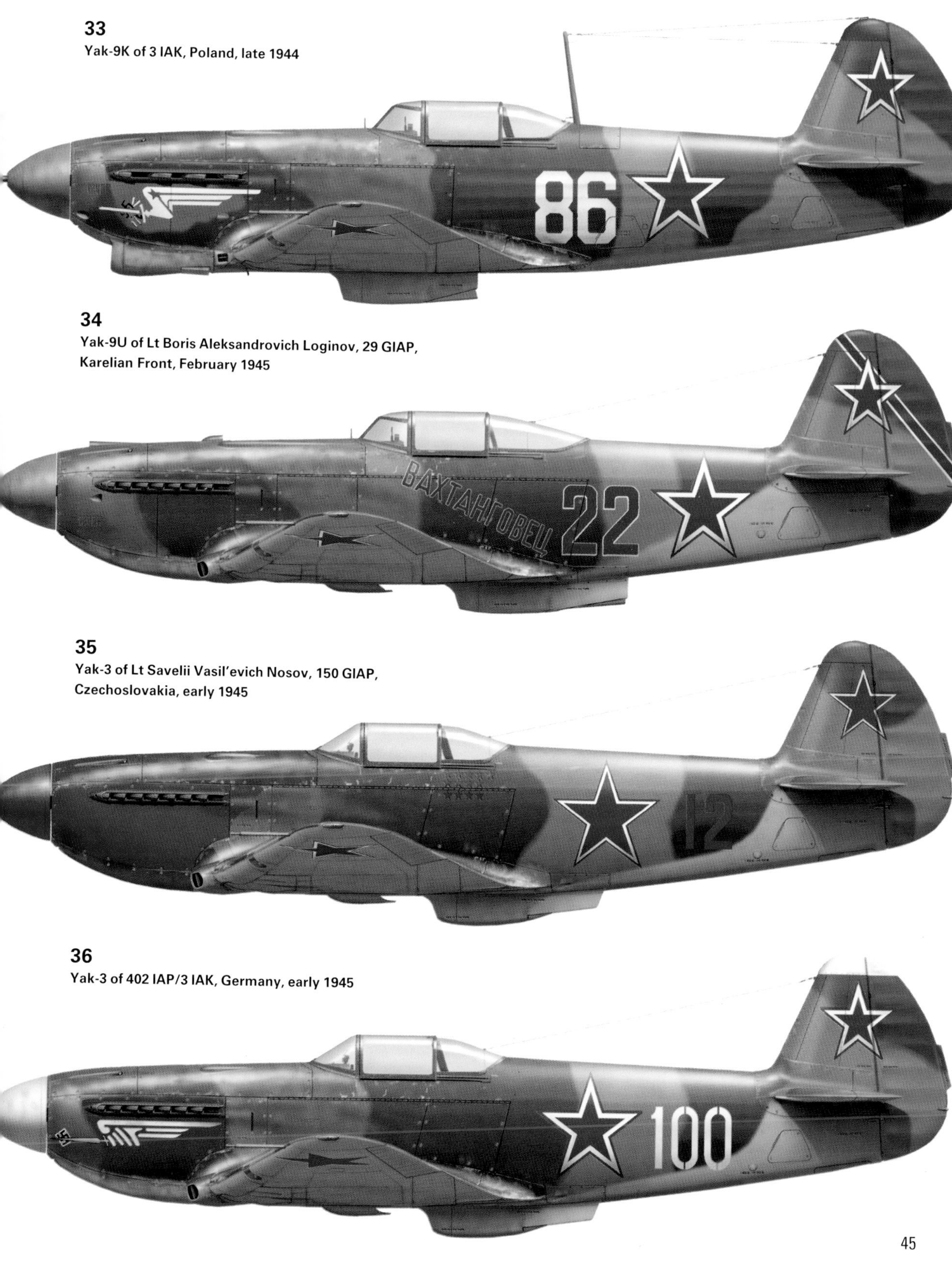


**33**
Yak-9K of 3 IAK, Poland, late 1944

**34**
Yak-9U of Lt Boris Aleksandrovich Loginov, 29 GIAP, Karelian Front, February 1945

**35**
Yak-3 of Lt Savelii Vasil'evich Nosov, 150 GIAP, Czechoslovakia, early 1945

**36**
Yak-3 of 402 IAP/3 IAK, Germany, early 1945

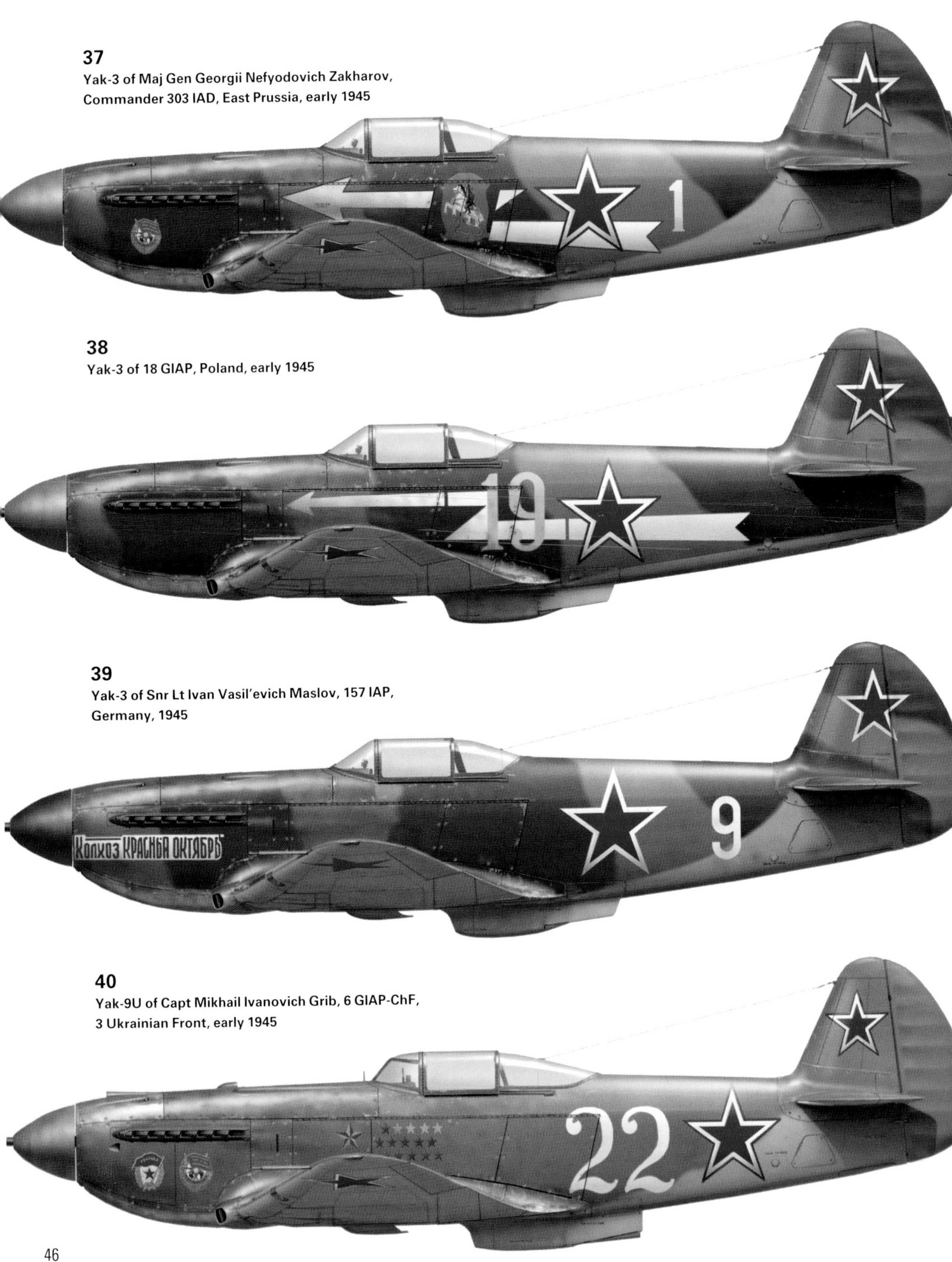


**37**
Yak-3 of Maj Gen Georgii Nefyodovich Zakharov, Commander 303 IAD, East Prussia, early 1945

**38**
Yak-3 of 18 GIAP, Poland, early 1945

**39**
Yak-3 of Snr Lt Ivan Vasil'evich Maslov, 157 IAP, Germany, 1945

**40**
Yak-9U of Capt Mikhail Ivanovich Grib, 6 GIAP-ChF, 3 Ukrainian Front, early 1945

inadvertently gained altitude and eventually reached 26,000 ft, where he passed out from lack of oxygen. When he came around again he found his fighter in a dive. Although he was able to recover, Baklan had ruptured his eardrums and damaged the airframe of his Yak so badly that he had to carry out a forced landing.

In April 1942 he was transferred back to 434 IAP, and on 23 July – his 25th birthday – Baklan downed a Bf 109, but was then attacked by three more Messerschmitt fighters and wounded in the arm. He escaped by diving away, and while fleeing at ground level he spotted one of his pursuers hit the ground while trying to follow him. In August Baklan was promoted to captain and made 2nd Squadron deputy CO. In September his unit was re-equipped with Yak-7Bs, and during his first flight in the new aircraft he shot down a Macchi C.200 fighter.

By October he had completed 400 sorties and scored 13 individual and 23 shared victories. Made a HSU on 23 November, Baklan had been appointed to the Fighter Inspectorate, along with fellow aces Dolgushin and Garanin, the previous month. He remained there for two months, before returning to 434 IAP with Vasilii Stalin in January 1943. They brought with them new Yak-9s, although the Yak-1 and Yak-7 were still used by the regiment.

In late 1943 Baklan was promoted to major and transferred to 19 IAP, operating Lavochkins. He flew the radial-engined fighter for the rest of the war, ending the conflict with over 700 sorties, 22 individual and 23 shared victories (15 and 23 were claimed with the Yak) to his credit.

Yet another famous pilot to join 434 IAP in 1942 was Capt Sergei Fyodorovich Dolgushin, who arrived on 16 September, having already been made a HSU four months earlier. Dolgushin had previously flown the I-16, MiG-3, LaGG-3 and Hurricane, and scored seven individual and four shared victories, plus four more which had been denied due to personal difficulties with a commissar. On the very day he joined 434 IAP on the Stalingrad Front, Dolgushin claimed a Ju 88 destroyed followed by a Bf 109 24 hours later.

On 19 September, the rear gunner of a Ju 88 damaged the engine of Dolgushin's Yak-7, but he was able to glide the fighter back to Soviet territory and make a belly landing. Two days later he was on patrol again in a new aircraft. In the morning he shot down a Ju 87, and in the afternoon his formation of 16 Yaks encountered 60 Bf 109s at an altitude of 10,000 ft. Both formations broke up in the dogfight which ensued, and Dolgushin was able to escape by diving into a cloud layer at about 2000 ft. When he came out of the clouds and attempted to regroup his formation to return home, he was bounced by two German aircraft. Avoiding their initial attack, Dolgushin counterattacked and shot down the leader, but he

**Maj Gennadii Mikhailovich Yakhnov, Deputy CO of 33 IAP, stands beside his Yak-7B in late 1943. Yakhnov served with this regiment throughout the war, scoring 12 individual and five shared victories. He was awarded the HSU on 22 August 1944 (*G F Petrov*)**

Capt Pavel Ivanovich Pavlov, CO of the 1st Squadron 21 IAP-KBF (Baltic Fleet), taxis out in his Yak-1 during the summer of 1942. By the end of the war he had scored 12 individual and five shared victories (eight and two with the Yak). Pavlov received the HSU on 5 November 1944 (*G F Petrov*)

was himself forced to bale out of his burning fighter. Landing in Soviet territory, his burns and a leg wound kept him out of action until late October, when he was assigned to the Air Force Inspectorate.

In January 1943 Dolgushin returned to his regiment, which had been redesignated 32 GIAP and placed under the command of Col Vasilii Stalin. Now equipped with a mix of Yak-7s and Yak-9s, the regiment was assigned to 210 IAD of 3 Air Army and based at Zaborov'e, south of Demyansk on the Kalinin Front.

Stalin generally flew as a member of Dolgushin's flight, which must have placed an additional burden on him. During this time there had been particularly heavy combat on the Kalinin Front, and Dolgushin increased his score by a further six victories. One was against a Fw 190, which he shot off Stalin's tail, and another was a Ju 88 downed on 9 March over his own airfield, and watched by Marshal Novikov. A third was a fighter shot down over the Lovat River crossing on 15 March. In May Dolgushin was transferred to 30 GIAP as deputy CO, and was later appointed 156 IAP CO. For the rest of the war he flew P-39s and Lavochkins, and by VE-Day his official score stood at 17 individual and 11 shared victories, of which ten had been claimed in Yaks.

Another 434 IAP pilot was Vladimir Aleksandrovich Orekhov, who joined the regiment in 1941. By the following March he was a senior

The battered remains of Sgt Vasilii I Tkachyov's Yak-1, seen after a particularly hard fought air combat on 11 September 1942. Tkachyov, who was assigned to 21 IAP-KBF, returned to base with minor wounds at the end of this sortie, although he had shot down a Fw 190 prior to being hit himself. Tkachyov, who was eventually promoted to captain, had scored 12 individual and eight shared victories by the time he was killed in action on 1 September 1944 (*G F Petrov*)

An unidentified naval aviation pilot reports back to his CO in 1942 (*G F Petrov*)

lieutenant, having flown 235 missions and claimed eight aircraft destroyed in the air and two on the ground. Orekhov was wounded in the arm and leg in early 1942, and only returned to the regiment at year-end.

During early 1943 he frequently flew in the same flight with Vasilii Stalin, and received the HSU on 1 May. He was also known for his proficiency on reconnaissance missions. By the start of 1944 Orekhov had been promoted to major and given command of one of the regiment's squadrons. By VE-Day he had flown 420 sorties and scored 19 individual and two shared victories, plus four destroyed on the ground.

Upon graduating from flying school, Vladimir Aleksandrovich Lutskii served as an instructor until June 1942, when he was posted to 434 IAP as a flight commander. He scored his first kill on 27 July 1942, and was later promoted to major and made a squadron CO. On 9 March 1943, while fighting over his own base, Lutskii downed a Ju 88 reconnaissance aircraft, together with both escorting Fw 190s. By June he had flown 135 missions and destroyed 11 aircraft, and he was awarded the HSU on 24 August 1943. Lutskii claimed five victories during the Battle of Kursk, and in May 1944 he assumed command of 32 GIAP, where he remained until war's end. He flew about 300 sorties in total and scored 20 victories.

Unlike a number of other early Yak regiments, 4 IAP inexplicably missed out on receiving Guards status, despite its tally of 439 victories establishing it as the tenth highest-scoring VVS regiment.

At the start of the war it was based near Kishinev, 4 IAP flying MiG-3s and Hurricanes in the Ukraine and south of Moscow until it received a mix of Yak-1s and Yak-7s in August 1942. Although it numbered many

Pilot's from 3 GIAP-KBF's duty flight man their lightened Yak-1 fighters at Alert 1 in the Leningrad area in the summer of 1942 (*G F Petrov*)

successful pilots among its ranks, 4 IAP's best known aces were Ryazanov, Pogorelov, Stepanenko and Shmelyov.

Also seen on page 49, lightened Yak-1s of 3 GIAP-KBF sit at Alert 1 in the Leningrad area in the summer of 1942. The pilots strapped into these machines are L P Savkin and I P Kucherov (*G F Petrov*)

High-scoring aces Sultan Amet-Khan, Vladimir Lavrinenkov and Ivan Borisov began their careers with 4 IAP, before transferring to 9 GIAP in November 1942. They all scored early kills with the Yak-1, but became better known flying P-39s and La-7s – their careers are covered in the volumes dealing with these aircraft in this series.

Graduating from flying school in 1939, Aleksei Konstantinovich Ryazanov spent his entire wartime service with 4 IAP, claiming his first victory on the day Germany invaded the USSR. After fighting for over a year in the MiG-3 and Hurricane, he started flying the Yak-1 in the late summer of 1942. At about this time Ryazanov was promoted to captain and given command of the 4 IAP's 2nd Squadron.

On 21 August, while escorting Il-2s, his formation of six Yak-1s was attacked by eight Bf 109s. In the ensuing battle he shot one of them down and followed this with a Macchi C.200 later in the day.

Ryazanov was one of the pilots selected for transfer to the elite 9 GIAP, but he declined the invitation, preferring to remain with his old regiment. In 1943 he was promoted to major.

Ryazanov scored no fewer than ten victories during the fighting over the Kuban in early 1943, three of these falling on 29 April alone. However, on his seventh sortie that day he was forced to take to his parachute when his Yak was shot up by the gunner of a Do 217 that he was pursuing. By the end of May Ryazanov had flown 300 missions and scored 16 individual and 16 shared victories in 67 combats.

Pilots from 3 GIAP-KBF listen to their political education officer during a mandatory lecture on the Leningrad front in the summer of 1942 (*G F Petrov*)

He continued to add to his score in early June when he attacked a squadron of Stukas that he discovered taking off. Quickly shooting one dow, Ryazanov was then shot up himself by a Bf 109. Although wounded, he managed to shoot down a second enemy machine before escaping eastwards. As he reached Soviet lines, his fighter became uncontrollable and Ryazanov baled out. Rescued by his own troops, he was sent to hospital for treatment to eye and head wounds. He received the HSU on 24 August 1943.

By the time Ryazanov was well enough to return to action, 4 IAP had re-equipped with Yak-9Ts. The regiment fought its way across Poland and into the Baltic region, and on 16 February 1945 he flew an escort mission over Tukums-Libau for Il-2s of 225 ShAP (Assault Air Regiment), which were challenged aggressively by Fw 190s. Ryazanov and his friend I N Stepanenko each downed a Fw 190. One of the two German pilots shot down on this date was the Luftwaffe's fourth highest scoring ace, Otto Kittel (267 victories), of I./JG 54.

On 25 February Ryazanov shot down his 31st enemy, but his Yak was hit by flak and he was wounded by shell fragments. The wounds were bad enough to keep him out of action for the rest of the war. Ryazanov's final wartime statistics were 509 missions flown and 97 air combats fought, during which he had scored 31 individual and 16 shared victories. He received a second HSU on 18 August 1945.

Fellow 4 IAP ace Mikhail Savel'evich Pogorelov graduated from the prestigious Kacha flying school just as the Germans invaded. He was posted to 4 IAP in late June 1941, but as a new pilot in a regiment with few aircraft left, he flew very little. He did score a few victories when the regiment received Hurricanes, however, although his success truly began when the regiment was re-equipped with Yaks in August 1942.

Pogorelov became a close friend of Ivan Stepanenko, with whom he had joined the regiment, and they often flew together as a pair. He is known to have shot down a Bf 109 in June 1942, and at least five aircraft during the battle for Stalingrad. It was while fighting over the outskirts of the city in the August battles that he was shot down and wounded, although he destroyed two Bf 109s before he baled out.

Pogorelov was soon back in action, and he accounted for further Bf 109s on 14 and 29 September while flying with Stepanenko, and downed nine battling over the Blue Line in the spring of 1943.

On 31 July he became deputy CO of the regiment's 2nd Squadron, even though his rank still was only starshina (master sargeant). By January 1945, when he was nominated for the HSU, Pogorelov had been promoted to captain and given command of a squadron. He had undertaken 218 combat flights and scored 18 individual victories, including one by ramming, plus five shared. Pogorelov also received the HSU on 18 August 1945. Although his final tally is uncertain, a good estimate would be 24 individual and five shared victories scored.

Undoubtedly the best-known 4 IAP ace is Ivan Nikiforovich Stepanenko, who was completing his flight training at Kacha when the Germans attacked. Formal exams were cancelled with the promise, 'they will be given at the front'! The students were all promoted to sergeant and sent off to the Southwestern Front. Stepanenko and several friends were assigned to 4 IAP, and he had few opportunities to fly until the beginning of 1942, when the regiment received Hurricanes. Stepanenko scored only a single victory in the Hurricane, and he was also shot down and wounded in one.

The highly decorated Yak-1B of Capt Vladimir Ivanovich Pokrovskii, who was assigned to 2 GIAP-SF (Northern Fleet), in late 1944. Pokrovskii scored 12 individual and six shared victories, and was awarded the HSU on 24 July 1944 (*G F Petrov*)

In June, the regiment converted to the Yak-7 and redeployed to the Stalingrad Front. Soon after its arrival, 4 IAP became embroiled in a major dogfight when 20 Ju 88s were intercepted. Stepanenko managed to shoot one down, but while still admiring the results of his handiwork, Stepanenko was bounced by Bf 109s and again wounded. A few days later he found himself fighting a lone battle against ten Bf 109s that were attacking his airfield. Stepanenko was again shot down and wounded, but not before accounting for one of his attackers.

On 7 September he shot down a Fw 189, followed by a Bf 109 one week later, and then another on 29 September. On 6 October, while flying a reconnaissance mission with his wingman, Stepanenko was bounced by four Bf 109s on the way home. His wingman's engine was hit and he had to force-land, leaving Stepanenko to fight on alone, while trying to make it home with the valuable film. Two Bf 109s fell in flames, but Stepanenko was also hit. Landing inside Soviet lines, he was able to remove the camera and return on foot with the film.

In the spring of 1943 4 IAP deployed over the Blue Line, and Stepanenko was promoted to senior lieutenant. In June 1943 the regiment converted to the Yak-9, and in the late autumn Stepanenko received a Yak-9T with a 37 mm cannon.

The regiment arrived too late for the Battle of Kursk, but it did participate in the subsequent counter-offensive. Throughout the autumn Stepanenko's score continued to grow, and he was promoted to command the 2nd Squadron as a captain. He spent much of spring 1944 in hospital having his old wounds treated, and was awarded the HSU on 13 April. Returning to combat in May, Stepanenko now found himself primarily flying escort missions for Il-2 *Shturmovik*, as well as the occasional free hunt.

Naval groundcrews re-arm the nose cannon in an unidentified Yak (*G F Petrov*)

From late 1944, 4 IAP operated over Kurland and East Prussia, where he scored most of his victories over Fw 190s from JG 54 – the last of these came on 7 May. By war's end Maj Stepanenko had completed 414 sorties and officially scored 33 individual and eight shared victories in 118 air combats, although he personally claimed 70 individual and 13 shared victories. He received his second HSU on 18 August 1945.

Il'ya Vasil'evich Shmelyov graduated from Borisoglebsk Flying

School in 1940 and was assigned to an active unit from June 1941. But his service appears to have been without distinction, and nothing is known of any accomplishments he made until April 1943, when he was sent (with the rank of major) to 4 IAP as commanding officer of its newly re-established 3rd Squadron.

Yak-9s, presumably of a naval regiment, fly over an unidentified coastline. The absence of a number on the nearest machine is unusual (*G F Petrov*)

On 27 April he began a run of victories by downing a Bf 109, followed on 29 and 30 April by eight more aircraft, including four Ju 87s in a single engagement. By May he had flown 198 missions, and in 35 air combats scored 14 individual and ten shared kills (ten of these were scored fighting over the Blue Line).

One of Shmelyov's victims was another Yak which had been terrorising VVS aircraft – it was being flown in Soviet markings by a German pilot who used this deception to gain close advantage. The Soviet high command devised an elaborate plan in which all Yaks on the front received two black bands painted on the fuselage by the tail. This enabled 4 IAP to hunt down the first Yak its pilots spotted without such markings, and Shmelyov was the pilot who scored the kill.

Awarded the HSU on 24 August 1943, the ace enjoyed great success in a Yak-9 over Riga during the Baltic campaign in October 1944. He scored another nine victories to take his total to 29 individual and 15 shared kills in 350 sorties and 77 air battles.

Another unit to gain fame flying the Yak was 6 GIAP-ChF (Black Sea Fleet), although its three most famous pilots began the war with neighbouring regiments.

Konstantin Stepanovich Alekseev joined the Navy in 1936 and graduated from Eisk Naval Flying School in 1938. Alekseev began the war as a senior lieutenant with 9 IAP-ChF, and on 17 October 1941 he and several other pilots were transferred to the 5th Squadron of Yak-1-equipped 32 IAP-ChF.

6 GIAP-ChF Yak-9Ds fly in close formation for the camera in the summer of 1944. Aircraft 22 was assigned to 17-kill ace Mikhail Ivanovich Grib. Note the Guards and Red banner emblems on the nose of Grib's fighter (*G F Petrov*)

In early 1942 this squadron was transferred to the decimated 8 IAP-ChF (6 GIAP from 3 April 1942) as the regiment's new 1st Squadron, and Alekseev became deputy CO. During the first half of 1942, Alekseev fought in the defence of Sevastopol. By April of that year he had completed 272 combat sorties and fought in 72 air battles, shooting down 11 aircraft. On 8 June Alekseev was seriously wounded when shot down, and he was evacuated to the North Caucasus. Six days later he was awarded an HSU.

Capt Mikhail Avdeev of 6 GIAP-ChF (Black Sea Fleet) by the tail of his aircraft in 1942. He survived the war with 17 victories to his credit (*G F Petrov*)

On the night of 19 April 1943 Alekseev shot down three He 111s, and by October of that year he was a major, and CO of Yak-1/7-equipped 25 IAP-ChF. Alekseev had flown over 500 sorties by VE-Day, including 50 ground attack and 60 reconnaissance missions. In 110 air combats he scored a total of 22 victories, eight of which were claimed at night.

Mikhail Ivanovich Grib was another pilot to begin the war flying with 9 IAP-ChF, although he transferred to the 5th Squadron of 32 IAP-ChF in October 1941 and then to 8 IAP-ChF (6 GIAP-ChF from April 1942) the following January. Against great odds, he gained four victories during the defence of Sevastopol, and by August 1942 had completed 250 sorties and scored ten victories in the Yak-1. Receiving the HSU on 23 October 1942, Grib continued to fly with 6 GIAP-ChF until war's end, by which time he had become CO of the regiment's 3rd Squadron. Grib flew 500 sorties and scored 17 victories, four of which may have been shared.

Snr Lt Mikhail Vasil'evich Avdeev was another pilot to follow the path from 9 IAP-ChF to 32 IAP-ChF and then to 8 IAP-ChF. It appears that on 25 October 1941, shortly after joining 32 IAP-ChF, Avdeev encountered leading German ace Hermann Graf. His Yak was badly shot up and Graf claimed him as his 17th victim, but in fact Avdeev managed to limp home with severe damage. On 23 January 1942 the tables were turned, and Avdeev claimed to have shot down the Bf 109 flown by Wolf-Dietrich Huy of III./JG 77. Although Avdeev was given credit for the victory, Huy actually managed to escape and make a successful forced landing.

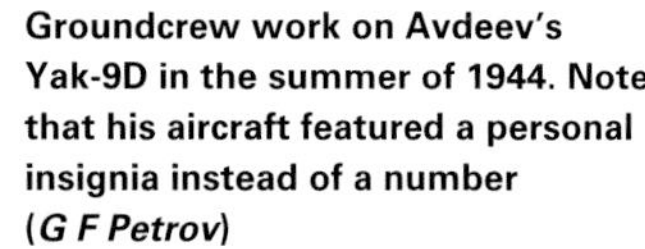

Groundcrew work on Avdeev's Yak-9D in the summer of 1944. Note that his aircraft featured a personal insignia instead of a number (*G F Petrov*)

Avdeev was awarded the HSU on 14 June 1942 for completing more than 300 missions and shooting down nine enemy aircraft. By May 1943 he had become regimental CO, and a year later he was promoted to lieutenant colonel. By VE-Day Avdeev had flown 498 missions, fought in 141 air combats and scored 17 victories.

# THE TIDE TURNS

Following the fall of Stalingrad in early 1943, the nature of the air war began to change as rapidly as the conflict on the ground. Now, the Yak-9 began to enter service in significant numbers, followed shortly afterward by the Yak-9T and other improved derivatives. New pilots arrived at the front who now began their careers flying the Yak-9 instead of outdated I-16s, Hurricanes and LaGGs. Others who had survived the first years of war, giving an honest performance, now began to produce dramatic results, and formerly undistinguished regiments became some of the most successful. Now these units deployed increasingly not just as regiments, but as divisions and even corps.

One of the most famous Yak aces, as well as the fighter's greatest advocate, was Twice Hero of the Soviet Union Maj Gen Evgenii Yakovlevich Savitskii, famed for his callsign 'Drakon'. By the end of the war he was commander of 3 Fighter Corps, but still flying fighter missions and scoring victories.

Savitskii had graduated from flying school in 1932 and then been sent to the Far East, where he commanded several units including 3 IAP, which had a bad reputation for poor discipline and even worse flying skills. Within the year, Savitskii had transformed it into the best regiment in the Far East. For this he was rewarded with his own personal vehicle, while all members of the regiment received gold or silver watches. Shortly afterwards Savitskii was promoted to colonel and appointed CO of 29 IAD.

He stayed in the Far East for most of 1941, but in November he was selected for temporary duty in the west and assigned to Col Sbytov, CO of Moscow air defence forces. Although Savitskii said he hoped to prove himself, and gain combat experience at the front, Sbytov reminded him that he was a divisional commander, and not just an ordinary pilot. Savitskii was ordered to study combat reports and documents to gain a better understanding of the war, and the lessons learned. Only after he had mastered staff duties, and thoroughly studied the combat reports, was he sent to a

**An unidentified pilot of Evgenii Savitskii's 3 Fighter Corps. Note the distinctive winged star behind him on the nose of his Yak. This emblem was added to all of 3 IAK's aircraft within weeks of Savitskii taking charge (*G F Petrov*)**

combat regiment. This experience was to prove a formative lesson for Savitskii's further career.

The regiment to which he was sent was commanded by Lt Col Samokhvalov, who was one of his former subordinates. The latter felt uncomfortable about having a divisional CO and senior officer who might not be able to look after himself in combat under his command. Savitskii explained that his whole division was equipped with the LaGG-3, which was flown by Samokhvalov's regiment, and that he was quite prepared to fly as a wingman until he gained experience.

The next day Savitskii flew his first combat mission in Samokhvalov's flight, the Soviet pilots intercepting a formation of Stukas, escorted by Bf 109s. In the ensuing combat, Savitskii saw a pair of Bf 109s moving on to Samokhvalov's tail, and he rushed to the attack. He fired his rockets at distance to distract them and then opened fire with his guns at too distant a range. The Germans wheeled around and came after Savitskii and his wingman. Realising his first combat mistake, Savitskii got onto the tail of the Bf 109 leader and held his fire until close range. His target broke up in front of his eyes. And then Savitskii made his second mistake – taking a moment to admire his work. The impact of a heavy shell on his seat armour informed him of his blunder, but his wingman chased the German from his tail. Savitskii had scored his first kill and learned two valuable combat lessons.

At the end of January 1942 Savitskii's temporary assignment expired and he went back to the Far East, before permanently returning to the west on 1 May. Promoted to colonel, he was appointed CO of the newly-formed 205 IAD.

On his arrival, Savitskii found his division equipped with a mixture of Yak-1s and P-39 Airacobras. He also discovered that most of his pilots wanted to fly the P-39 rather than the Yak. Savitskii was amazed that

**Four pilots from Savitskii's 3 IAK return from a mission. Although the second pilot from left appears to be very young, he has already won three medals. The aircraft appear to be late model Yak-7Bs (*G F Petrov*)**

Soviet pilots would prefer to fight in a foreign aircraft instead of one designed and built in their native land. He decided to make his point with a practice duel against the best of the Airacobra pilots, which he won. He persuaded his pilots that the Yak was superior, but would later have less luck in convincing leading P-39 ace Aleksandr Pokryshkin. Savitskii exclusively flew Yak fighters for the rest of the war.

His greatest contribution in combat was as a tactician and teacher. One of his important achievements was introducing the concept of a loose and wide-ranging escort for *Shturmoviks*, instead of the customary close one, which he felt robbed the fighters of initiative against the enemy. In doing so, Savitskii reached the same conclusion as Adolf Galland and, later, pilots of the US Eighth Air Force. Another innovation was to replace the old three aircraft V-formation with pairs and fours at a time when it was still being strongly resisted by most Soviet units. At the end of December 1942 Savitskii was ordered to relinquish his command on the South-western Front and report immediately to VVS headquarters in Moscow.

Poor weather conditions made it impossible to fly in a transport aircraft, and as for rail travel, 'walking would be quicker'. Savitskii decided to fly in a captured Fieseler Storch, but when he arrived in Moscow, ahead of schedule, the weather was bad there too. Unable to find the central aerodrome, Savitskii landed in a convenient open space – the frozen Moskva River near the Kremlin's Crimean Tower. Yelled at by a policeman, Savitskii explained his circumstances and, after receiving directions, arrived at his correct destination.

Half an hour later he was received by Gen A V Nikitin, representative of the VVS Staff. Nikitin had heard about his flight in the Storch, and denounced him as 'childish, irresponsible to fly in an unknown enemy aircraft in such weather' and much worse. Nikitin added, 'And you aren't listening to what I'm saying!' Savitskii stood wondering why he had been summoned from the front, where every fighter pilot was needed. Nikitin eventually finished his tirade, concluding with 'and, by the way, it has been decided to appoint you commander of a fighter aviation corps – 200 aircraft under your command. The corps, as a part of the Supreme High Command Reserve, will be used to achieve air superiority'. Savitskii was also promoted to major general.

As the air corps came under STAVKA (Headquarters of the Supreme High Command) control, rather than being an organic part of an air army, Savitskii's units would be shifted from front to front. His corps subsequently took part in the battles over the Kuban, Ukraine, Crimea, Belorussia, the Baltic and the final assault on Berlin.

Savitskii's 3 IAK was allotted the experienced 265 and 278 IADs, which were reforming after extensive combat. Although both divisions were led by experienced aviators, most of their pilots were new. Savitskii immediately met with his two divisional commanders, followed by the six regimental commanders and finally the squadron COs. Savitskii insisted on a practice air duel with each commander to assess his strengths and weaknesses in his most vital function.

During the first months of 1943, Savitskii's IAK was withheld from combat while its regiments undertook thorough intensive training. Savitskii made significant use of a captured, airworthy Bf 109 to give his pilots actual experience against enemy aircraft before meeting them in

Four pilots from Savitskii's 3 IAK pose with a Yak-3. Note that each man is wearing a different style of flying kit, and that the pilot on the left has acquired a German flying helmet! Also note the different style of winged insignia on the fighter's nose (*G F Petrov*)

combat. Later on, when 3 IAK entered combat, Savitskii adopted the practice of regularly selecting new and inexperienced pilots to fly as his wingmen on combat sorties, trying to take as many novices as possible to give them combat experience and confidence. As a way of boosting morale and aiding identification, Savitskii had special winged insignia painted on the noses of all corps aircraft.

The high command decided to send 3 IAK to 4 Air Army, operating over the Kuban, but before departure, Savitskii was summoned to the Kremlin for a personal meeting with Stalin, who stressed the importance of his new assignment.

Savitskii flew on the corps' first mission on 20 April 1943, providing air cover for the Soviet beachhead at Mount Myskhako. During that day the corps destroyed 47 German aircraft, one of which was shot down by the CO himself. But a week later, Savitskii's Yak-1 was shot down by a Stuka

Capt Georgii Sergeevich Balashov was a squadron commander with 3 IAK's 402 IAP. He received the HSU on 1 July 1944 after scoring 15 victories, and may have achieved more kills before the end of the war. Note the 3 IAK insignia on his Yak-3 (*RART*)

gunner and he was forced to parachute into the Black Sea. He was soon rescued by a motor launch.

These Yak-3s are also identified as belonging to 402 IAP. The identity of the pilot in the foreground is not known, but the number of the nearest machine suggests that it might belong to the regiment commander, since 100, like 1, was sometimes adopted by the CO. If so, this could be 20-kill ace Maj Anatolii Ermolaevich Rubakhin (*G F Petrov*)

In September Savitskii showed another sort of courage when he defended some of his pilots who had been unjustly accused by the Air Army commander, Gen Goryunov. I V Fyodorov of 812 IAP was sent to intercept bombers attacking Kiyachenko's Cavalry Corps, but his flight was bounced from above by the fighter escort. Two Yaks were lost and no victories scored, while the German bombers conducted a punishing raid on Soviet cavalry. An incensed Goryunov had both Fyodorov and the regimental CO brought before a tribunal, which sentenced them to lengthy terms of imprisonment, stripped them of rank and sent them to a penal battalion. When he learned of this, Savitskii championed their cause, taking the case to Air Army headquarters at no small risk to himself.

Ultimately, the part of the sentence expelling the accused and consigning them to a penal battalion was lifted, and they were allowed to remain in the corps. By the end of the war the sentence had been reversed and the prison terms cancelled, as both officers had repeatedly distinguished themselves. From then on Savitskii often selected Fyodorov to fly as his own wingman as a demonstration of confidence.

Ivan Vasil'evich Fyodorov graduated from flying school in March 1941, but was sent to the Far East. He remained there until late 1942, when he was sent to 812 IAP, which became one of the best regiments in Savitskii's corps. With the Yak-1, Fyodorov flew his first sorties over the Kuban in April 1943, and scored his first victory on 20 April. The engagement fought that day was a fiasco, however, as the inexperienced squadron broke formation while attacking Ju 87s and was bounced by the escorts. Seven Yaks were lost, although they also claimed seven Ju 87s and four Bf 109s destroyed. Six days later Fyodorov shot down a Fw189, but was again bounced by the escorts. This time he had to crash-land his Yak.

On 10 May Fyodorov was returning from a sortie in one of the regiment's six remaining aircraft with fuel and ammunition low when he was bounced by six Bf 109s. He shot down one of his attackers, but when his own Yak was set on fire, he rammed a second Messerschmitt and then baled out. In three weeks Fyodorov had scored six victories, but had also been shot down twice. His regiment then stood down to re-equip with Yak-9s, and on 26 September Fyodorov shot down three bombers in a single morning mission, but in the afternoon he got into trouble with Gen Goryunov, as previously recounted.

In early 1944 Fyodorov received a Yak-9T, with which he scored 15 victories. He also flew the Yak-9K, with an even larger 45 mm engine-mounted cannon. By August 1944, Fyodorov had flown 285 missions, and in 62 air combats had shot down 24 aircraft, with a further nine destroyed on the ground. On 21 September he was promoted to captain, and became an HSU on 26 October. That autumn Fyodorov's regiment converted to Yak-3s.

The next major Soviet operation commenced on 12 January 1945, and by early February 812 IAP was based at Reppen, just 60 km from Berlin. On 4 February the regiment was attacked by three waves of Fw 190s, including two groups of Fw 190Ds, one of which was shot down by Fyodorov. In March, while flying in a foursome with Savitskii, he shot down another Fw 190 when they became involved in a fight against large numbers of fighters escorting a pilotless Ju 52/3m 'flying bomb'. Fyodorov's last victory was again an Fw 190, shot down over Berlin on the night of 20-21 April.

By war's end he had flown 416 missions, including 180 reconnaissance and 84 ground attack sorties. In 104 combats, he scored 36 victories, plus one shared, and destroyed nine aircraft on the ground.

By March 1944 units in Savitskii's Corps had been mentioned in Supreme High Command dispatches 21 times. Savitskii had personally flown 107 sorties (including those as an air division commander) and shot down 15 aircraft. During the operation to seize the Crimea, Savitskii had also started operating with some of the first field-deployable radar units in an effort to better maintain air superiority over the front.

**Capt Abrek Arkad'evich Barsht poses with his groundcrew and a sharksmouthed Yak. Flying various Yak-1s with an artillery spotting regiment, Barsht scored eight personal victories and was awarded the HSU on 10 April 1945 (*G F Petrov*)**

**This pilot (at right) is unknown, but his aircraft displays an interesting personal insignia on its nose. He appears to be meeting an official delegation (*G F Petrov*)**

During the liberation of the eastern Crimea in mid April 1944, Savitskii discovered three abandoned Bf 109s in good condition at Veseloe airfield. He decided to use them for reconnaissance over German rear areas, intending to fly these missions himself. Indeed, he told 8 Air Army CO, Gen Khryukin, that he was the only pilot in the corps who knew how to fly the Bf 109. After several unconventional and dangerous flights, including one which ended with Savitskii being captured by his own side on landing, he was forbidden to continue flying the aircraft on pain of removal from command. After a few days' consideration, Savitskii decided that if nothing went wrong, he could escape detection, and the consequences. Besides, if he did come down behind enemy lines, removal from command would be the least of his problems.

On 11 May 1944 while flying his Yak over the last German stronghold in the Crimea, Savitskii's aircraft was shot up by a Bf 109 and its tail damaged. As he attempted to return home, he was hit again, this time by flak. While belly-landing his fighter behind German lines, he suffered a compression fracture of three vertebrae. With difficulty, Savitskii managed to evade capture and return to Soviet lines. There, he was captured by Soviet infantrymen, who refused to believe that the scruffy looking pilot in the tattered flight suit was a general. In fact, everyone was mistaken. Savitskii was no German, but neither was he a major general – returning to his headquarters, he was informed that he was now a lieutenant general and an HSU as well!

After the liberation of the Crimea, 3 IAK was redeployed to 3 Belorussian Front for Operation *Bagration*. The advance was rapid and the battle lines were often confused to the point where, on one occasion, Savitskii got to experience ground fighting for himself. Meeting the general commanding a nearby mechanised cavalry group, the latter unit's headquarters suddenly found itself surrounded by German troops. However, as the enemy approached on motorcycles and trucks, they were annihilated by anti-aircraft batteries protecting the headquarters.

On another occasion a group of German parachutists was dropped near Savitskii's airfield, and again he and his men had to engage in hand-to-hand combat until the enemy was defeated. From spring 1944, Savitskii and his corps began to fly the Yak-9, although the division remained equipped with a mixture of Yak-7s, Yak-9 sub-variants and even some Yak-1s. In July Savitskii, with Lt M E Pivovarov as his wingman, flew a

**A squadron of donation aircraft is received by an unidentified unit at an official ceremony. The aircraft are inscribed *Kurskii Kolkhoznik* ('Kursk collective farmers') (*G F Petrov*)**

A close up of one of the Yak-9s seen in the photograph on page 61. Here, collective farmers meet the regiment's pilots at the conclusion of the donation ceremony (*G F Petrov*)

Yak-7B on a reconnaissance mission. Although they were engaged by 12 Fw 190s, both pilots were aces, and the Yak-7 was more manoeuvrable at low altitudes. Savitskii downed one fighter and Pivovarov damaged two more while keeping Savitskii's tail clear.

Sen Lt Mikhail Evdokhimovich Pivovarov was another to spend the first half of the war guarding the USSR's Far East borders against a possible Japanese attack. Only in September 1943 did he reach 402 IAP within Savitskii's 3 IAK. By war's end Pivovarov had flown 300+ sorties and scored 26 individual kills. He was awarded the HSU in May 1946.

In November 1944 Savitskii's corps was withdrawn into reserve and the regiments converted entirely to the new Yak-3, before being redeployed to strengthen Rudenko's 16 Air Army for the assault on Germany. Although the offensive opened on 12 January 1945, the weather prevented flying for the first two days. It then improved enough for a limited number of flights to be made, and on 18 January, while flying a free hunt mission with his wingman, Savitskii encountered 12 Fw 190 *jabos*. He attacked, downing one and disrupting the formation.

In late March Savitskii was flying with one of his favorite wingmen, Semyon Samoilov, when he spotted a twin-engined aircraft that appeared to be too small to be a bomber, and which he first took to be a Bf 110. But it was moving far too fast, and it glistened silvery-grey in the sun. He attacked with a burst of fire, but was unable to hit it, allowing the enemy aircraft to escape. Back at base, examination of the gun camera film revealed it to have been one of the Luftwaffe's new Me 262 jets.

Many other new weapons were now being deployed by the hard-pressed Germans. Savitskii was flying near Küstrin with Samoilov and I V Fyodorov and his wingman when they saw a large group of Fw 190s escorting a lone Ju 52/3m, which was obviously a very important target. Savitskii headed straight for the transport aircraft. He closed in and was about to open fire when he had to turn sharply to avoid two Fw 190s on his tail. Savitskii's flight shot down two of them, after which the others broke off combat and fled, leaving the Ju 52/3m to fly on and alone. After a while it dived into the ground and erupted in an unusually large explosion – the aircraft had been filled with explosives and set on its course on autopilot, after which the pilot had baled out. Had Savitskii shot it down, the explosion would probably have blown him out of the sky. Shortly afterwards, other pilots engaged *Mistel* fighter-bomber combinations .

**This photograph poses a problem. The aircraft's inscription declares *To Hero of the Soviet Union Klimenko from the collective farmers of Red Ossetia*, but the official listing of Soviet Heroes does not include any fighter pilot by that name. One possibility is that Klimenko might have got into trouble and been stripped of his awards after the war. The forward-slanting radio mast indicates that he is flying a Yak-9M (*G F Petrov*)**

By the end of the war Savitskii had found the time to fly 216 missions on top of his command and administrative responsibilities. He scored 22 individual and two shared victories. His last kill was a Fieseler Storch, which he shot down near the Tiergarten on 27 April 1945, although this victory was not included in his official score because it was an unarmed aircraft. On 2 June 1945 Savitskii received a second HSU.

In post-war Germany, Savitskii, still seeking an outlet for his aggression, suggested staging mock aerial combats with the Allies, or even football matches, but his ideas were poorly received. But one day in June 1945, while Savitskii was flying to a conference, his Yak-3 was bounced by a British Tempest whose pilot was obviously seeking duel. Taking up the challenge, Savitskii outmanoeuvred his assailant and three times sat on his tail in a killing position. Unfortunately, when he landed he was severely upbraided by Marshal Rudenko, who accused him of 'aerial hooliganism', no matter how much Savitskii insisted that 'the other chap had started it'. Marshal Zhukov was equally angry, and Savitskii was relieved of his command.

Shortly afterwards, though, he was summoned to headquarters and informed that Comrade Stalin wanted to speak to him on the telephone. After hearing Savitskii's explanation, Stalin asked about technical details – how did the British aircraft perform, and which fighter was better? He was delighted when Savitskii described the outcome of the duel, and stated that the Soviet fighter was indisputably superior to the British one.

In post-war years, Savitskii oversaw the introduction of jet fighters into the VVS, was duly promoted to Marshal of Aviation. By the time he

**Capt Mikhail Semyonovich Mazan flew this ferocious-looking Yak-9 while serving as an 85 GIAP squadron CO. He scored 19 individual and two shared victories before he was shot down and killed over Budapest on 12 December 1944. He received the HSU posthumously on 15 May 1946 (*G F Petrov*)**

stopped flying on 1 June 1974, he had accumulated 5586 sorties and 12,943 hours of flight time, of which 1201 were at night.

Many other famous aces were assigned to Savitskii's regiments, including Spartak Iosifovich Makovskii, who graduated from flying school at Kacha in 1939 and was sent to the Far East. In early 1943 he was assigned to 3 IAK as a senior lieutenant, leading a 43 IAP squadron. On 19 April 1943 the regiment returned to action over the Kuban, and Makovskii scored his first kill on 3 May. Five days later he destroyed a Bf 109 by ramming it with his wingtip during a head-on attack, the future ace returning to base with a damaged fighter. By January 1944 he had flown 92 sorties, scored 18 individual kills and one shared in 49 combats.

On 3 January, while attacking a German airfield at Bol'shaya Kostromka, he and his wingman, Lt I G Kuznetsov, each destroyed a Bf 109 on the ground. But Kuznetsov's Yak was hit by flak and he had to make a forced-landing before reaching friendly lines. Makovskii saw several trucks full of enemy troops approaching, so he landed his fighter under fire, rescued his wingman and took off again with Kuznetsov half in and half out of the cockpit, hanging on for dear life. German troops continued to fire at them as they chased the fleeing Yak.

Makovskii was awarded the HSU on 13 April 1943 and promoted to major. He subsequently scored additional victories, including two kills over Berlin on 19 April 1945 and a pair of Fw 190s on the 29th for his final successes. Makovskii's score is listed as either 30 victories or 23 individual and one shared victories in 218 sorties and 79 air combats.

Snr Lt Konstantin Petrovich Komardinkin graduated from flying school in 1939 and was posted to the Far East. He was subsequently sent to Savitskii's 3 IAK in 1943, being assigned to 274 IAP. Komardinkin scored his first victory on 29 April, and by October he had flown 90 missions, shot down 18 enemy aircraft and destroyed three more on the ground in 35 combats. He was awarded the HSU on 1 November, and the following April Komardinkin was promoted to captain and made a squadron CO. He failed to return from a mission on 17 April 1944 after scoring his 19th victory (an Fw 190).

The combat record of Jnr Lt Vasilii Sergeevich Konobaev illustrates the intensity of air combat. He graduated from flying school and was sent directly to the front in March 1942. After scoring a single victory, he was shot down and wounded near Stalingrad. Following his release from hospital, Konobaev was assigned to 291 IAP in Savitskii's corps. Between 20 April and 3 June 1943, he flew 56 missions and scored 17 individual and two shared victories in 35 combats. He was killed in action on 18 September 1943 and awarded the HSU posthumously on 13 April 1944.

Georgii Nefyodovich Zakharov was already an 'old man' of 33 when the war broke out, and he was also an experienced ace. He had learned to fly in 1930, and in October 1936 was part of the first contingent of fighter pilots to fly in Spain, where he scored six victories. Within six months of returning home he was off again, this time to China, where he scored three more kills. By June 1941 Maj Gen Zakharov was CO of 43 IAD, based in the Western Military District and comprising four regiments equipped with I-16s and I-153s.

In the months after the German invasion, Zakharov's division was repeatedly destroyed, rebuilt and destroyed again, while Zakharov

Gen G N Zakharov, in flying helmet, discusses plans with Maj Khustinskii and aces Joseph Risso (of the Normandie Regiment) and Maj Ivan Aleksandrovich Zamorin in front of the general's Yak-3 in 1945. A man who led from the front, Zakharov completed 153 sorties and scored ten kills in 48 air combats during World War 2. These were added to his 11 pre-war victories in Spain and China. Zakharov was awarded the HSU on 19 April 1945 (*G F Petrov*)

himself scored three more kills. Although lucky to avoid being among those to face a firing squad in punishment for this catastrophe, Zakharov was nevertheless removed from command and posted to a series of training assignments. In December 1942 he was finally given command of the newly-formed 303 IAD, which comprised the Yak-equipped 18 GIAP and 168 IAP, as well as 523 IAP, flying the La-5. Later, 168 IAP was replaced by 20 IAP and 9 GIAP, and the French Normandie Regiments were added.

From now on, most of Zakharov's time was consumed by administrative tasks, but he still managed to go hunting. On these occasions he used either a La-5 or a Yak-7, depending on which regiment he flew with. In early 1943, plagued by Army complaints about the hated Fw 189 *ramas*, Zakharov summoned the commander of 18 GIAP and the commander and navigator of 523 IAP and they went hunting in pairs. Zakharov bagged his *rama*, and so did the other pair.

While many Soviet generals commanding air divisions flew combat missions, and some became aces, Zakharov was the only one to take an enemy pilot prisoner. On 13 June 1944 he flew to Zaol'sha, where 18 GIAP was based, arriving soon after the regiment's CO, ace A E Golubov, had taken off on a sortie. Observed by his visitors, Golubov attacked two Bf 109s and shot down one of them – a fate which befell a Ju 88 moments later.

Seeing the Messerschmitt pilot bale out, Zakharov and ace I A Zamorin jumped into the regiment's Po-2 hack and set off in an attempt to prevent him from escaping. He was still in the air when they arrived, and they landed moments after the pilot touched down. He was duly captured and disarmed. However, the Po-2 had become stuck while landing, and Zakharov and Zamorin had to force their prisoner to help them push its tail out of the mud. When they flew him back to the airfield, they were greeted by Golubov, who reported his two kills, and was surprised to be presented with the captive pilot by his visitors.

In September 1944, when 18 GIAP and Normandie converted to the Yak-3, Zakharov adopted the type as his own mount. The division's 139 GIAP (formerly 20 IAP), meanwhile, received Yak-9Us.

In October Zakharov's division returned to the front in East Prussia, where it served for the rest of the war. He remembers 16 October 1944 as

The lightning bolt and ornate numbers reveal this Yak-7 to be an aircraft of 18 GIAP, and that the photograph was almost certainly taken in mid 1943. The pilots' identities cannot be determined, however (*G F Petrov*)

the division's most successful day, because that was when it shot down 56 enemy aircraft for no loss. Of the total, 18 GIAP scored 19 victories and Normandie-Nieman 29, and during the month the division accumulated 184 victories. Its last air combat came on 12 April 1945 with a claim for 13 victories.

18 GIAP's origins lay in 6 IAP, which was transferred from the Far East in July 1941 and used Polikarpov fighters during the war's first months. In early 1942 it was split into two regiments. One became 18 GIAP on 7 March and flew Yak-1s and later Yak-7s. Confusingly, the other unit retained its 6 IAP designation until July 1944, when it became 149 GIAP.

The first CO of 18 GIAP was Maj Sergei Ivanovich Chertov, who had been commissar of 6 IAP on the outbreak of war – a flying commissar was unusual. Chertov scored his first victory in July, and in August he claimed three more, before becoming the regiment's CO. He led 18 GIAP until October 1942, when he swapped commands with 523 IAP CO Maj Anatolii Golubov. Chertov spent the rest of the war flying Lavochkins, and ultimately scored 15 individual and seven shared victories. It seems likely that about six of these were claimed while flying Yak fighters.

Graduating from flying school in 1933, Anatolii Emel'yanovich Golubov was wounded in action in late June 1941. After his release from hospital, he was sent on a course for regimental commanders, and in June he went to LaGG-3-equipped 523 IAP, before taking command of 18 GIAP in October 1942. While not a prominent ace, Golubov was an inspirational commander of a regiment which ended the war with 427 victories, over half of which were achieved under Golubov's leadership.

On 28 June 1944, during Operation *Bagration*, the Red Army badly needed information on German troop movements. With experienced pilots having already failed to penetrate enemy territory because of dreadful flying conditions, Golubov decided he would have to fly the mission himself – alone. Flying very low, he obtained the vital information, radioed his report and turned for home as the weather started to improve.

**A Yak-3 of 18 GIAP waits for its next sortie on a captured German airfield in early 1945 (*G F Petrov*)**

Yak-3s of 303 IAD sit victoriously on another German airfield in early 1945. It is impossible to tell if they are from Normandie or one of the other regiments within the division (*G F Petrov*)

He then encountered a pair of Bf 109s and attacked them. He shot down the wingman, but while chasing the second fighter, Golubov's Yak was hit by flak and set on fire.

Flying at just 200 ft, he was too low to take to his parachute, he decided to use the 'sryv' method of aircraft evacuation in which the pilot deployed his parachute while still in the aircraft, allowing the slipstream to pull him out of the cockpit. As he escaped, Golubov's Yak exploded. He regained consciousness on the ground, surrounded by Soviet infantrymen.

At first it appeared that he would not survive, and although his condition improved, doctors believed that he would never fly again. However, by the end of September, Golubov had left hospital and returned to the regiment, which was now flying the new Yak-3. Golubov spent three days converting onto the aircraft, and on 6 October he resumed command of 18 GIAP. In January 1945 Golubov left to become Deputy CO of 303 IAD. During the war he flew 355 missions, and in 43 air battles scored 10-14 kills. He was awarded the HSU on 29 June 1945.

The officer who commanded the unit in Golubov's absence, and again after his departure in January 1945, was Maj Semyon Alekseevich Sibirin. In 1943 he had led the regiment's 1st Squadron, and during the fighting for Smolensk had scored six victories. In early 1944 he was promoted to major, and became the regiment's deputy CO. By June 1944, having raised his score to 18, Sibirin was appointed temporary CO. He was awarded the HSU on 1 July 1944 for 246 sorties and 17 individual victories and one shared in 36 air combats. When he assumed command of the regiment, however, Sibirin had less opportunity to fly – although he still managed a few more flights. During one, on 16 October 1944, he shot down a Fw 190 over Insterburg. A final victory claim on 13 April 1945 brought his score to at least 20 individual victories, plus one shared.

Another of 18 GIAP's outstanding aces was Capt Nikolai Grigor'evich Pinchuk. Although he had joined the VVS in 1940, he was assigned to training units until October 1942, when he joined 18 GIAP as a sergeant pilot and went to the front in 1943. His first victory was scored in the spring over a Ju 88 reconnaissance aircraft, which he shot down at an altitude of 26,000 ft. On 29 August he shot down a He 111, and the next day he destroyed another Heinkel bomber in the morning, followed by a Stuka shot down and a second rammed in the afternoon. Pinchuk was then forced to bale out, and a Fw 190 tried to strafe him in his parachute. He was saved by Albert Durand of the Normandie regiment. This episode cost Pinchuk a month in hospital, but when he returned he was promoted to captain, and given command of the 1st Squadron.

By the beginning of 1945 Pinchuk had flown 226 missions, fought 46 air combats and scored 18 victories, including one by ramming. He was awarded the HSU on 19 April 1945.

The Germans continued to resist in East Prussia, and on 1 February 1945, while Pinchuk was flying with his wingman Nikolai Kornienko at 13,000 ft, he met six of the latest and newest Bf 109 variants. Kornienko manoeuvred the Germans down to a lower altitude, where the Yak-3 regained its superiority, and they each shot down one of the new fighters. When they returned to base, their encounter was of great interest to VVS intelligence officers. By war's end Pinchuk had completed 307 sorties and scored 22 victories, plus two shared, in 68 air combats.

Another outstanding unit was 4 GIAD. Transformed from 274 IAD on 13 March 1943, it comprised three regiments – 271, 653 and 875 IAPs, which became 64, 65 and 66 GIAPs. The first two regiments began the war flying old aircraft, receiving Yak-1/7s in 1942. Despite being a Guards regiment, 875 IAP retained the Yak-7B well into 1943, and only converted to the Yak-9 in the autumn. In late 1944 it received Yak-3s.

One of 271 IAP's leading aces was Pavel Ignat'evich Murav'yov, who graduated from flying school in 1938 and first saw combat against the Finns in 1939-40 – he flew 94 sorties and was credited with a Gladiator and two Blenheims shot down. In October 1941 Murav'yov was posted as a flight commander to 271 IAP, which was equipped with the I-16 and LaGG-3, before converting to the Yak-7 in 1942. By February 1943 he had flown 185 sorties and scored nine individual and five shared kills. He was nominated for the HSU, which he received on 1 May 1943.

Murav'yov had one of his most successful days in March 1943, when the Soviets began an offensive near Demyansk and Velikie Luki. On 15-16 March the Germans opened a major aerial counter-attack against the Lovat River crossing. These were opposed from first light on the 16th by Murav'yov, who led a patrol of six Yak-7s to cover the bridgehead in the Ramushovo-Kobylkino region. Encountering eight Fw 190s, they shot down six for no loss, one of which was credited to Murav'yov.

At midday he went back to the same area, leading a patrol of eight Yak-7s. At between 8000-10,000 ft, they saw a formation of 18 Ju 87s,

**Capt Aleksandr Nikolaevich Kiloberidze of 65 GIAP is seen in his Yak-9 in the Polotsj region of Belorussia in June 1944. The inscriptions read *For Brother Shota* and *To the west* (G F Petrov)**

**This Yak-7B has been provisionally associated with 42 IAP, but the use of a scroll with crossed-out swastikas suggests that it could belong to 3 GIAD, which was the only other unit known to display such a device (*G F Petrov*)**

escorted by ten Fw 190s and four Bf 109s, approaching the bridgehead. Again, Murav'yov claimed one of the six aircraft shot down, which were achieved without loss. That evening he led a third patrol of eight Yaks back over the river crossing, where they fought with six Fw 190s. They shot down three fighters, and again one was claimed by Murav'yov. None of the Yaks were lost in return. That day Murav'yov had claimed three victories, and his pilots another dozen. They had suffered no losses, and had prevented the bridgehead from being disrupted. This performance helped earn the regiment Guards status (as 64 GIAP) on 18 March 1943.

During the Battle of Kursk, the unit was based on the northern side of the bulge, near Orel. On 12 July 1943 Murav'yov led a patrol of six Yak-7s, which caught eight Bf 110s and six Bf 109s attempting to attack Soviet tanks. Murav'yov downed two, while his pilots claimed three.

By the end of the war Murav'yov was a lieutenant colonel and deputy CO of 64 GIAP. He had flown 473 sorties and scored 37 individual and five shared victories in 149 air combats.

Viktor Yakovlevich Khasin was in combat from June 1941, and by late 1942 he was a senior lieutenant and deputy squadron CO with 271 IAP. During the first year of the war he flew primarily ground attack sorties, as air combat involved not so much scoring kills as avoiding becoming one. By late 1942 things had begun to change, however. On 3 December, while leading a flight over Velikie Luki, he observed a formation of six Ju 88s with a fighter escort. Manoeuvring to attack out of the sun, Khasin downed a bomber and led his flight away from the escort without loss. Minutes later they encountered a lone Do 217, which he also destroyed.

By March 1943 he was commander of the 1st Squadron, but that same month he was wounded in an air battle and crash-landed his Yak-7 in a forest. For two days Khasin was unable to leave the crash site, and his legs became frozen before he was rescued. Although he returned to the front on his release from hospital, it was to a different unit. While serving with 271 IAP, he had flown 659 sorties and fought 257 air combats, scoring ten individual and five shared victories. He was also credited with a further eight aircraft destroyed on the ground.

Awarded the HSU on 1 May 1943, Maj Khasin was killed on 14 January 1944. All told, he had completed more than 700 sorties and fought more than 300 air combats. His final score was 13 individual and five shared aerial kills, plus eight aircraft destroyed on the ground.

Nikolai Denchik's career, and possibly his life, was saved by the arrival of a dedication aircraft in his name (*G F Petrov*)

Dedication and gift aircraft were a source of pride for their recipients. But for ace Capt Nikolai Fyodorovich Denchik, his was a true lifesaver. Denchik had flown in combat since June 1941, and by December 1943 he was a senior lieutenant and commander of 64 GIAP's 1st Squadron. He had completed 63 sorties and scored 13 individual and three group victories in 18 air combats. He was awarded the HSU on 4 February 1944, and shortly afterwards was promoted to captain. With the award of the HSU, Denchik went on a brief leave, and was able to return to his home in the town of Manchenki. When he left, pride in their native son led the people to collect funds to buy him a dedication Yak-3. Arriving in the autumn of 1944, it saved him from serious difficulties.

During Operation *Bagration*, I GIAK, of which 4 GIAD's 64 GIAP was a component, was assigned to 3 Belorussian Front. The Soviet advance was so rapid that numerous German units were cut off, nearly intact, behind Soviet lines, much to the surprise of both sides. At the same time Soviet rear support units and aviation bases struggled hard to keep up with the advancing front. Fighter units often based themselves just behind the frontlines, and so were frequently in danger. Near Minsk, 3 and 4 GIAD encountered a German infantry force fighting its way westwards through Soviet lines. Having managed to evacuate its aircraft, 3 GIAD was able to organise a successful perimeter defence of its airfield. Things did not go quite so well for Loshintsa-based 4 GIAD, however.

On the night of 6 July the Germans subjected the airfield to a severe artillery bombardment, which killed four men and wounded 23. It also destroyed six aircraft and damaged 20 more. The bombardment was followed up by an infantry assault, which penetrated the airfield perimeter. Seeking to preserve his aircraft, Denchik took off under fire in a Yak-9 – the only pilot to succeed in doing so. He strafed the enemy and flew to a safe landing field. Meanwhile, the groundcrews and other pilots improvised a perimeter defence until Soviet tank units arrived and the Germans surrendered. The regimental staff was seriously compromised by its failure to provide adequate security or reconnaissance. It had also panicked under attack, and lost control of the situation. Now it was looking for scapegoats.

Instead of interpreting Denchik's feat of taking off at night under fire as an act of bravery, they called it cowardice and planned to haul him up before a tribunal. By the time it was convened, Denchik's donation aircraft had arrived for presentation. As the political officer argued, Denchik was a Hero of the Soviet Union with numerous victories, so what could they say to the good people of Manchenki? The matter was quietly forgotten, at least by the authorities if not by Denchik, and he was even promoted to major in early 1945. By the end of the war he had completed 534 sorties and scored 19 individual and three group victories in 120 air combats.

Vasilii Nikolaevich Kubarev qualified as a flight instructor at an aero club and then studied to become a doctor. But pilots were in demand, so he returned to flying and graduated from an Air Force flying school at the end of 1939. Although Kubarev volunteered for the front in June 1941, he was retained as an instructor until November, when 653 IAP was formed from instructors at his Armavir Flying School. Kubarev was appointed commander of the 3rd Squadron, but the regiment was condemned to fly the I-15bis, which had been declared obsolete three years earlier. The aircraft were committed to the defence of the Crimea, and since they were hopeless for air combat, they were used for ground attack, with two 100-kg bombs or RS-82 rockets hung beneath the wings.

Despite this inferiority in numbers and equipment, Kubarev managed to shoot down a Bf 109 to score the regiment's first aerial victory in early 1942. On 8 May, the unit was surprised during lunch when German tanks appeared on the airfield. Pilots had to evacuate their aircraft across the straits to Taman. Soon afterwards, the depleted regiment was sent back to Saratov to re-equip with the Yak-1.

In early October 1942, 653 IAP (65 GIAP from March 1943) returned to action, joining 274 IAD on the Kalinin Front. Based at Staraya Toropa, and participating in the battles around Kholm and Velikie Luki, the regiment initially had to fly defensively while its pilots became familiar with the Yak. However, in December, they began to achieve successes, and on the 15th Kubarev claimed one of the regiment's early victories.

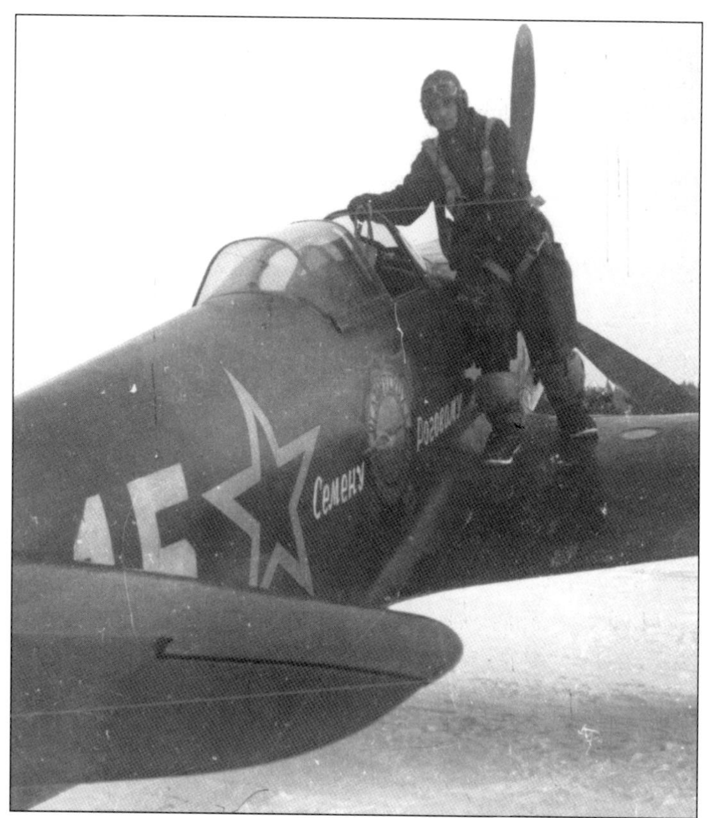


**This Yak-3 was presented to Lt Semyon Rogovoi of 64 GIAP by sailors of the Amur River Flotilla in the Far East. What he did to merit this honour is not known, since there is no indication that he ever scored a single victory (*G F Petrov*)**

Returning from escorting a reconnaissance Pe-2, he was ordered back into the air just as his wheels touched the runway. Ju 88s had been spotted approaching the airfield. Gunning the motor of his Yak, Kubarev gained altitude. He had enough ammunition, but barely sufficient fuel. Attacking head-on against the formation leader, he aimed at the bomber's right engine and fuel tank. The Ju 88 was hit, began to burn and fell to earth. The formation scattered and the raid was disrupted. Kubarev ran out of fuel soon after landing.

Several weeks later Kubarev suffered a serious leg wound following an accident with a pistol. This kept him out of action for three months, but on 8 June 1943 he shot down a Fw 190, which was attacking an airfield near Orel. He downed another fighter on 11 June.

**The inscription on this Yak-3 reads** ***To the fighter pilots the 3rd aircraft from the woman collective farmer, A S Selivanova of the Named for the 7th Session of the Soviets of the Kurilovskii District, Saratov Region*****. Neither the pilot's identity nor that of the unit which received this aircraft is known (*****G F Petrov*****)**

As Kubarev's Bryansk front was to the north of the main Kursk battlefield, he scored only two victories before 12 July 1943, when the Orel counter-offensive was opened. At 0510 hrs the whole regiment assembled in formation, complete with Guards banner, to hear attack orders and speeches by the commander and political officer, both of whom stressed the importance of the assault. At 0600 hrs the regiment took off to begin a day in which it was to fight ten air combats and score five victories, two by Kubarev.

The next day Kubarev was leading six Yaks when he spotted a small formation of two Ju 87s and four escorting fighters below him. This was very much at odds with standard German tactics so Kubarev was cautious. He left Popov's pair above while he and Khitrov attacked from the left, with Gus'kov's pair coming in from the right. Kubarev's burst sent one of the Stukas down, and he saw the other vanish into a cloud. Just then, above him, he spotted a much larger formation – 27 Ju 87s, with 20 Fw 190 escorts.

He ordered Popov and Gus'kov to take on the bombers while he engaged the escorts. In the fight that followed, Gus'kov downed two bombers, while Kubarev and Khitrov, using a vertical manoeuvre, destroyed two Fw 190s. They were unable to occupy them all, however, and Popov could not get at the bombers, although he did down a third Fw 190. When their fuel was nearly exhausted, Kubarev's formation broke off combat and returned to base without loss. Some 25 years later, Kubarev recalled this engagement as his most memorable of the war.

During the battle for Orel, 65 GIAP scored 68 victories, of which 32 were credited to Kubarev's 2nd Squadron. By August 1943 he was a major, with 114 sorties, 53 air battles and ten aircraft shot down to his credit. Kubarev was awarded the HSU on 28 September 1943, and a few months later he was appointed the regiment's deputy CO.

The opening day of Operation *Bagration* (22 June 1944) also saw the liberation of Belorussia and the destruction of German Army Group Centre. After taking part in the initial phase of the Belorussian operation, 65 GIAP was redirected northwards in late July for the liberation of the Baltic region. It continued to fly over this area until April 1945, when it took a short break to convert to the Yak-3, before turning towards the northern flank of Berlin.

By the end of the war Kubarev had flown about 300 sorties. Most sources credit him with 46 victories, but he told the author that he had scored only 18 individual kills, and that the rest had been shared. He is even more proud of his unit's score of 371 victories. This high proportion of group kills suggests a leader who was responsible, and concerned, for the success of his men and his unit more than his own personal accomplishments. He retired with the rank of colonel general and still lives in St Petersburg.

Andrei Petrovich Chernobai was at the front from June 1941, and he flew with 875 IAP from the summer of 1942. By the following January he was a deputy squadron commander, having flown 90 missions and scored 11 individual and 27 shared victories in 40 air combats. Chernobai was awarded the HSU on 22 February 1943 and promoted to captain. He was subsequently withdrawn from combat and reassigned as a test pilot.

Sergei Danilovich Luganskii first saw combat during the Winter War against Finland in 1939-40, flying 59 sorties. He destroyed a Gladiator and was himself shot down behind Finnish lines, although he managed to escape capture. Many contradictory reports surround Luganskii's activity during the first months of the war, one account stating that he was strafed in his parachute. Another claims that the regimental commissar was shot down during a mission and SMERSh (the KGB's assassination division) arrested Luganskii, handling him quite roughly until eventually absolving him of blame.

Luganskii's combat history does become clearer from late 1942, however, by which time he was already serving with LaGG-3-equipped 270 IAP. He scored a few victories, but only after the regiment converted to the Yak-1 in early 1943 did his career begin to blossom. By August of that year Luganskii had flown 221 sorties and scored 18 individual victories, plus one shared. He received the HSU on 9 September 1943 (a second followed on 1 July 1944).

**Sergei Luganskii poses with the Yak-1B purchased for him by the people of Alma-Ata in the spring of 1944 (*G F Petrov*)**

In the early autumn, while protecting the Dnepr River crossing, Luganskii rammed a He 111, destroying its rudder with his propeller. The bomber went down and Luganskii was able to return to base. The whole incident was watched by Air Force CO, Marshal Novikov.

By December 1943 Luganskii had shot down another 13 aircraft, but that same month he and his wingman were bounced in the landing circuit of their airfield by two

**Luganskii and his specially built Yak-1B. The inscription reads *To Hero of the Soviet Union Sergei Luganskii from the Komsomolists and youth of the city of Alma-Ata* (*G F Petrov*)**

Luftwaffe 'free hunters'. The wingman avoided the first attack and shot down one of the Germans, but was then killed himself. Luganskii survived himself by lowering his landing gear and reducing his speed to such a degree that the bullets missed and the German fighter overshot him. On the verge of stalling, Luganskii was forced to retract his gear and turn, and this time the German pilot did not miss. The Yak's windscreen and instrument panel were smashed and Luganskii was hit in the leg.

Attempting to gain height for a third pass, the Bf 109 pilot was caught out by the speed of Luganskii's virtually fuelless Yak. The Soviet pilot soon caught up with the Messerschmitt, got onto its tail and sent it down with a burst of fire in its engine.

Recuperating, Luganskii returned home to Alma-Ata, where the citizens bought him a new Yak-1B. It was not just an ordinary production

**9 GIAP's double HSU winners Vladimir Lavrinenkov (left), who scored 16 of his 36 individual and all 11 shared victories in the Yak-1, and Pavel Golovachyov, who claimed ten of his 31 individual victories, plus one shared, in the Yak-1, receive their Communist party cards from Commissar Nikolai Verkhovets in January 1943. These pilots scored all of their Yak-1 success between October 1942 and August 1943 (*G F Petrov*)**

aircraft, but an airframe specially produced for Luganskii by the Saratov factory with individual improvements and particular care taken in its construction. The dedication markings were applied at the factory.

In May 1944 he became CO of his regiment, which had become 152 GIAP on 5 February 1944. In March 1945 Luganskii was withdrawn from combat and sent to the Air Force Academy. By this time he had flown 390 sorties and scored 38 individual and six shared victories.

Arsenii Vasil'evich Vorozheikin never intended to be a pilot. In 1932, after completing two years of service in the cavalry, he began studying to become a journalist. However, in 1934 the Soviets began a major air-mindedness campaign, and his local Communist Party chapter ordered Vorozheikin to volunteer for military flying training. In 1939 he saw his first combat against the Japanese at Khalkin Gol, where he flew 160 sorties, fought 30 air combats and scored six individual and 12 group kills. Shortly afterwards, Vorozheikin flew against the Finns in the Winter War. At the end of the Finnish campaign he was sent to the Air Force Academy and then to the Transcaucasus to patrol the borders with Turkey and Iran.

In September 1942 Vorozheikin was assigned to 728 IAP – a battered regiment still flying obsolete I-16s. He quickly proved himself and was appointed CO of the 2nd Squadron, but although Vorozheikin was able to complete his escort missions, he was unable to score any victories with the Polikarpov fighter. In March 1943 the regiment was pulled back to re-equip with the Yak-7, returning to the front on 10 July 1943 with the Battle of Kursk at its height. Thrown into action, Vorozheikin soon shot down a Bf 109G-2 for his first victory since 1939. Despite this success, within four days his entire regiment had been reduced to only eight Yaks.

On 14 July Vorozheikin led a formation of four Yak-7s against wave after wave of Stukas, with Bf 109 escort. He shot down two of the dive-bombers, and each of his companions downed one apiece, but then his Yak was hit. With his cockpit growing warmer by the minute and smoke pouring in from the engine, Vorozheikin hastily turned for home. When he tried to bale out, however, he found the canopy was jammed. Fortunately, he succeeded in reaching a forward airfield and landed safely. Just two bullets had hit his fighter, one holing the radiator and the other jamming the canopy. Following this experience, Vorozheikin removed the canopies from all of his fighters from then on, despite being told that this increased drag and degraded performance.

On 4 August 1943, Vorozheikin was leading six Yak-7s over Tomorovka when they encountered a large force of Ju 87s, and their escorts. He duly shot down three Stukas and a Bf 109, while his pilots accounted for more of the German aircraft. Two Soviet pilots were shot down and a third badly wounded.

By late October 1943 the battle to liberate Kiev was raging, and on

**Posing for the camera at Rovno in December 1943 are, from left to right, Sergei Lazarev, Arsenii Vorozheikin (46 kills in World War 2), Mikhail Sachkov and mechanic D Mushkin of 728 IAP. Lazarev scored 22 individual and three shared victories and was awarded the HSU before his death over Bunslau on 1 March 1945. Sachkov scored 26 victories and also won the HSU (*G F Petrov*)**

**The identity of this pilot is unknown, but there are at least 18 victory stars and a most peculiar emblem partially visible on his Yak (*G F Petrov*)**

**This insignia was applied to a Yak-1B of an unknown regiment (*RART*)**

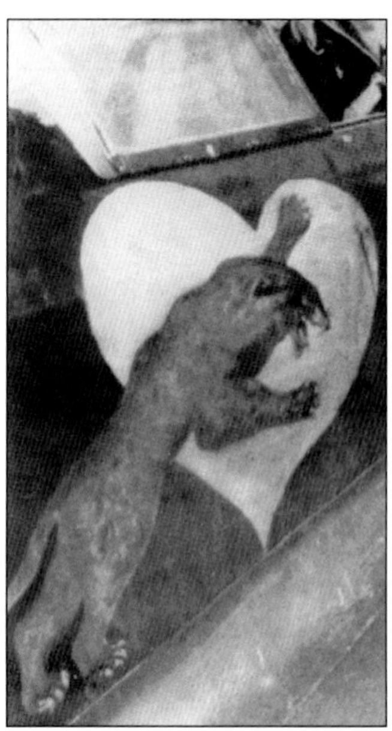

4 November Vorozheikin and his wingman each shot down a Fw 190. The next day fellow ace Igor Kustov suggested that the regiment should paint the noses of its aircraft red as far back as the cabin. This was to serve as a red banner, just like those the ground forces carried into action, and it also marked the 26th anniversary of the revolution and the liberation of Kiev, which was just days away. The city was liberated 48 hours later.

Flying west of Kiev in his newly red-nosed Yak-7, Vorozheikin again engaged the Germans, and shot down another Fw 190. He noted that this was his 13th kill of the war, all of which had been scored in just four months since 10 July. Ten had been achieved during the battle for Kiev.

On 4 February 1944 Vorozheikin was to receive his first HSU. Two months earlier 728 IAP had converted to the Yak-9D, Vorozheikin's being equipped with a camera for photo-reconnaissance sorties. In early February 1944 the regiment returned to a frontline base near Zhitomir.

Vorozheikin not only flew frequent reconnaissance sorties in his Yak-9D, but he had also acquired a dangerous habit of photographing the remains of his dogfight victims. On 28 February 1944 Vorozheikin was scrambled to deal with a Fw 189 and two unknown types bombing Soviet troops north of Lutsk. When they arrived, the unknown types turned out to be Henschel biplanes, one of which Vorozheikin shot down. He decided to fly low and capture his victim on film, but was surprised by an intense barrage of small arms fire from a nearby wood, which damaged his aircraft. He turned for home, but the engine in his fighter seized and began to burn, necessitating a wheels-up landing 40 km from the front. The regiment picked him up in a Po-2.

In March 1944 the new L'vov-Sandomir offensive opened, and 728 IAP was redeployed to Zubovo airfield in the Carpathian foothills. A large German force had been surrounded as a result of the Soviet offensive, and the Nazis responded by attempting an airlift with their remaining transports. They usually attempted to fly at night, or just before dusk, and on one occasion in early April Vorozheikin caught a large formation of Ju 52/3ms. Closing in on a pair of transports, he shot them both down, but his radiator was hit in turn and he was forced to head for home. As he did so, Vorozheikin radioed an order to his mechanic to prepare another Yak so that he could catch the Ju 52/3ms on their return flight. Although the aircraft was ready, he was unable to take off again because night was fast approaching.

Vorozheikin was at the controls of a Yak-9T when he next encountered the enemy, and he shot down three more Ju 52/3ms near Ternopol. While returning to base he spotted a Ju 88 reconnaissance aircraft. Vorozheikin was concerned about his lack of ammunition, but he attacked anyway using his single machine gun to aim before firing the fighter's 37 mm cannon. There was only a single round left in the latter, which hit the Ju 88, but seemingly produced no result. Then, suddenly, fire broke out and the aircraft rolled over and crashed.

In early May 1944 Vorozheikin was wounded on the ground when a German bomber made a surprise attack on his airfield. Although he jumped into a trench, the ace was hit by several bomb fragments and spent the next two months in hospital. On release in July, Maj Vorozheikin was reassigned to his division's 32 IAP as deputy CO, but the regiment was withdrawn to the reserve almost immediately.

On 19 August, a Li-2 transport arrived at 32 IAP's airfield bearing a major from headquarters with news for Vorozheikin that he had just been awarded his second HSU – he had also been awarded the Distinguished Flying Cross by the United States.

By the end of September 1944 Vorozheikin had completed 300 missions and shot down 40 aircraft in 90 combats. He was known for helping younger pilots gain experience, and was responsible for aiding the careers of other successful members of his regiment. In October 1944 he was appointed Senior Instructor Pilot for Combat Preparedness of Frontal Aviation, which meant flying with various regiments and passing on his experience and skills to the newest generation of pilots.

In April 1945 Vorozheikin was flying a Yak-3 attached to 7 GIAD headquarters on 1 Ukrainian Front, which was closing in on Berlin. During a flight over the German capital, he managed to shoot down an Ar 234 jet bomber, although the kill was not officially recognised because the bomber's crash was obscured by the smoke of the city.

A few days later, on 1 May, Vorozheikin and his fellow instructors flew as an honour escort for the fighters of 115 GIAP, which dropped the red banner on the Reichstag. All told, he had flown about 400 sorties and scored 46 victories, in addition to his six individual and 13 shared kills from Khalkin Gol.

Aleksandr Ivanovich Vybornov graduated from flying school in 1940, but was retained as an instructor until October 1942, when he was sent to 728 IAP and adopted as wingman by Arsenii Vorozheikin. He was unable to score a victory until the regiment converted to the Yak-7B, however, claiming his first on 13 July 1943 when he shot down a Ju 87 over Kursk. Vybornov followed this up with a double kill the following day. In September he switched to the Yak-9, and by the end of the year had 21 victories to his credit. Promoted to senior lieutenant, Vybornov ended the war flying a Yak-3 over Prague. By then he had flown 190 sorties, participated in 42 air battles and scored 23 individual and four shared victories. He received the HSU on 27 June 1945.

Vybornov remained in the service post-war, and in 1967 he went to Egypt as head of a Soviet advisory group. There, he flew 15 air strikes against Israeli armour, as well as reconnaissance missions over Tel Aviv in the MiG-25R.

Aleksandr Ivanovich Koldunov graduated from flying school in 1943 and went to the front in May with 866 IAP, entering combat on 1 June. By mid July he had scored his fifth kill. Not long afterwards, his own Yak-9 was shot up. Koldunov was wounded and he had to make a forced landing in a cornfield. By the autumn of 1943 he had scored his tenth victory, earning him promotion to senior lieutenant and appointment to the 3rd Squadron as its CO. It may have been coincidence, but shortly after Koldunov became a squadron commander,

**728 IAP 27-kill ace Aleksandr Vybornov stands beside his Yak-9T in 1944. The inscription on his aircraft reads *Pupil of Kashir* (*G F Petrov*)**

Snr Lt Ivan Vasil'evich Maslov (right) flew with 157 IAP and scored 22 individual and 19 shared victories. He is seen here receiving a donated Yak-3 from the Red October Collective Farm. The P-39 in the background is curious since that type is not known to have been operated by this regiment (*RART*)

the performance of the regiment as a whole increased dramatically.

During the Belgorod and Izyum operations in autumn 1943, the regiment scored 171 victories, losing only six pilots to combat and non-combat causes. Koldunov was known for his analytical mind, his careful attention to the theory of air combat and his role as a teacher.

On 4 May 1944 he was leading six Yak-9s in an escort mission when 16 Ju 87s were spotted preparing to bomb Soviet tanks. He led the attack, shooting down two Stukas, while his flight claimed three more. By May 1944 he had completed 223 missions, scoring 15 individual and one shared kills in 45 combats. He was promoted to captain and awarded the HSU on 2 August 1944.

At the end of the summer 866 IAP converted to the Yak-3, which Koldunov flew for the rest of the war in battles over Rumania, Yugoslavia and Hungary. On 7 November 1944 he was involved in an inadvertent combat between Soviet Yaks and P-38s of the USAAF's 82nd Fighter Group, Fifteenth Air Force. Due to a navigational error, the Lightnings had attacked a Soviet armoured column north-west of Belgrade. They were then attacked by the covering Yaks of 659 IAP, with Koldunov's unit sent aircraft to assist. Before the pilots were able to establish identities and end the fight, both sides had suffered losses. The Soviets claimed to have shot down four P-38s for the loss of three Yaks and two pilots, while the US admitted losing three Lightnings, but also claimed three victories. Three of the claimed P-38s were credited to Koldunov, although they were not listed in his official score.

On 23 November Koldunov downed three fighters in a single sortie while protecting a river crossing. In the fighting over Hungary and Austria between 19 January and 13 April 1945, he scored no fewer than 22 kills in 29 sorties, and on 17 April he claimed three more Bf 109s. Koldunov's last kills came over Vienna when he shot down two long-nose Ta 152s or Fw 190Ds.

By VE-Day Koldunov had flown 412 sorties, fought 96 air battles and scored 46 individual kills, plus one shared. He received his second HSU on 23 February 1948. Post-war Koldunov eventually became Chief Air Marshal and CO of the PVO and Deputy Defence Minister. In May 1987 he was relieved of his command after Mathias Rust landed a Cessna 172 in Red Square.

Taken at the same time as the photograph above, this shot shows Maslov standing beside the nose of his new aircraft. These photos were probably taken before 1 July 1944, as the ace is not yet wearing his HSU medal, although the Guards badge on his tunic indicates that he had served with a Guards regiment prior to joining 157 IAP (*RART*)

# SPECIAL PILOTS

Among the thousands of pilots who flew Yaks were three groups which deserve a special mention, even if few of them became aces. The first comprised foreign pilots. After the Spanish Civil War a number of Spanish communist sympathisers escaped to the Soviet Union, where they joined a contingent of Spanish children who had been evacuated from Spanish Republican cities to escape the bombing. Following the German invasion, these refugees were eager to resume the fight, and those who were pilots joined the VVS. They were integrated into regular units – generally PVO regiments – but did not achieve many victories. Some of them flew Yak fighters, although none appears to have become an ace.

Antonio Garcia Cano flew the I-16 in Spain, but it is unclear whether or not he scored any victories there. During World War 2 he flew with Yak-1-equipped 573 IAP, and is known to have scored at least four and perhaps as many as six victories, including a He 111 shot down on 12 October 1942. Jose Pascual Santamaria, who scored three victories before he was killed in October 1942, probably served with the same regiment.

A far more notable group of foreign Yak fliers were those who served with the French Normandie Regiment, which began operations during the summer of 1943 as an independent squadron and eventually grew to regimental size. These pilots gained an outstanding reputation, and established themselves among the leading aces of both the French and Soviet Air Forces. They flew as a component of Zakharov's 303 IAD alongside 18 GIAP. Starting with the Yak-1, they moved onto the Yak-9 and then became one of the earliest units to receive the Yak-3. The detailed attention these pilots deserve can be found in the companion title *Osprey Aircraft of the Aces 28 - French Aces of World War 2.*

In mid 1944, 1 Polish IAP 'Warsaw' was established with the Yak-1 and sent to fly with 6 Air Army. Although the regiment received Yak-3s in early 1945, its pilots spent most of their time either escorting Il-2s of 3 Polish ShAP or providing air support for the Polish 1 Army. They saw little air combat and scored at most a handful of victories.

The most notable Polish pilot was Wiktor Kalinowski (Viktor Kalinovskii). He had been born in Ukraine in 1919 to Polish parents and grew up as a Soviet citizen of Polish nationality. After service as an artilleryman during the Finnish War, he attended flying school and became a fighter pilot. Assigned to 233 IAP, Kalinowski had scored eight victories by the time he was shot down and wounded in early 1942. Following his release from hospital, he was sent to 153 IAP (later 28 GIAP), where he flew the Yak-1 and Airacobra.

In the summer of 1944 Kalinovskii's Polish heritage became an asset when Stalin decided to create a communist Polish Air Force under Soviet influence. Since the Poles preferred to fly with the Royal Air Force, the Soviets were forced to recruit pilots of Polish or West Ukrainian origin who could pass as Poles. Kalinowski was appointed CO of 1 PLM (1 IAP)

Warsaw, which was initially equipped with the Yak-1B and later the Yak-9. On 19 April 1945, while he was flying with Lt Chromego as his wingman, he shot down two Fw 190s, and six days later he accounted for another.

This late model Yak-7B was apparently flown by Vasilii Stalin during his time as CO of 32 GIAP in early 1943. Unfortunately, the inscription on the fuselage is not clear enough to be read (*RART*)

All told, Kalinowski flew 215 sorties during the war and fought 139 air combats, scoring eight individual and four shared victories. Of this total, 90 sorties, including 28 ground attack missions, were flown with 1 PLM, as well as five of his combats and two individual victories, plus one shared. After the war Kalinovskii chose to make his home in the USSR.

In addition to the Warsaw Regiment, the Soviets also established Polish 3 Fighter Division with 9, 10 and 11 IADs, but these formations did not go into combat. Similarly, 17 Air Army's 236 IAD provided a basis for establishing three regiments of a revived Yugoslav Air Force, equipped with the Yak-9. But by the time the Yugoslavs were ready to fight, the Germans had been expelled from the Balkans, and they flew a few ground support missions at most. Likewise, the Bulgarian Air Force received Yak-9s after switching to the Allied side in 1944, but again they arrived too late for them to see any significant wartime activity.

Another group of special Yak pilots were the sons of the top Soviet elite. In those days, the sons of the privileged in all major countries used their influence not to gain exemption from military service or to seek safe sinecures, but rather to get dangerous assignments in which they could bring honour to their family names and possibly glory to themselves. Randolph Churchill served with the commandos, Americans with names like Roosevelt and Kennedy featured among the rolls of honour, and Benito Mussolini's son Bruno was lost while flying a combat mission.

Even though the communists apparently held such bourgeois sentiments in contempt, the sons of Stalin, Khrushchev, Mikoyan and others sought adventure, and to prove themselves in service.

As in Nazi Germany and Fascist Italy, from the late 1920s the USSR made a fetish of aviation as a symbol of modernism and 'working class power'. The Air Force duly became the most politicised and most fashionable branch of the military. Naturally the communist elites gravitated to aviation in a further demonstration of its appeal for adventurous people. Yet despite their daring, and their desire for it to be otherwise, these young members of the elite were often protected.

One of the first to choose aviation was Vasilii Stalin, the dictator's younger son, who graduated from the premier Kacha flying school in 1940 as a lieutenant. Others soon followed. Stepan was the oldest son of Anastas Mikoyan and nephew of the aircraft designer. Valentin Yaroslavskii's father Emelyan was one of Stalin's chief lieutenants and Timur Frunze's father had been a heroic commander in the civil war and commander of the Red Army in the 1920s until his death during a botched surgical procedure in 1925.

During the war Stepan Mikoyan's younger brother Vladimir, and Lev Bulganin, son of Khrushchev's future Defence Minister, also became fighter pilots. Leonid Khrushchev was also a pilot, but he was assigned to fly bombers.

Vasilii Stalin watched over the careers of his friends and ensured they were assigned to Yak fighter units. In late 1942 he managed to have himself appointed CO of 32 GIAP, which had been transferred to the Kalinin Front after being re-equipped with a mix of Yak-1Bs, Yak-7Bs and some of the first Yak-9s. Although Stalin was undisciplined and irresponsible, as well as a remarkably poor commander, he was also personally brave and recognised as a remarkably skilled pilot. He flew only 27 sorties, but that was due to circumstances beyond his control.

Stalin's older brother, Yakov Dzhugashvili, was an artillery captain who had been captured during 1941 and was shot after his father refused German offers to exchange him for an officer of equivalent rank. With the loss or severe wounding of several other of the elite sons during 1942, Lavrentii Beria decided that no more could be sacrificed. He instructed the Air Force commander to issue an order forbidding Vasilii Stalin from flying any more combat missions, not only over occupied but also friendly territory.

But during his 27 sorties, Stalin showed common sense, and in the air he only led the second pair in Sergei Dolgushin's flight. In air combat, skill and experience was everything, even for the regiment's CO and the dictator's son. Vasilii Stalin scored one individual victory (an Fw 190) and four shared (another Fw 190 and three Junkers bombers). On one occasion he was saved only when Dolgushin shot a German fighter off his tail, and he arrived home with 14 bullet holes in his aircraft.

The climax of Stalin's career came at the end of March 1943 when 32 GIAP stood down for re-equipment. After landing at the rear-area airfield, Vasilii led a fishing expedition down to the Selizharovka River using RS-82 rockets. About a half-dozen pilots and officers participated, including several HSU aces. The technique involved removing a rocket's fins, starting the 22-second delay fuse, throwing it into the river and then hauling in the stunned fish that floated to the surface.

The first few rockets worked according to plan, but the fuse on the fourth was defectively short and it blew up prematurely in the hands of the armament officer. He was killed instantly, while 16-kill ace Aleksandr Kotov received a stomach wound that was so serious that he had to be retired from the military in 1943. Vasilii was also wounded in the heel by shrapnel.

Partly as a result of this misadventure, and partly from a paranoid suspicion that several instances of careless aircraft maintenance in the regiment might be due to sabotage, Iosif Stalin removed Vasilii from command and forbade him from receiving any new assignment without the Commander-in-Chief's approval. Later in the war, Vasilii was given command of 3 GIAD, although he was not allowed to fly combat.

In January 1942 Stepan Mikoyan was sent to 11 IAP, which was based at Moscow's Central Airfield mainly undertaking ground strafing missions. On 16 January Mikoyan few his eleventh sortie. His formation leader spotted a Ju 88 reconnaissance aircraft and ordered Mikoyan to move in and claim his first kill. But as he did so, Mikoyan was shot down by another Yak from a neighbouring unit, which mistook him for an escorting German fighter. Mikoyan crash-landed his burning fighter and was rushed to hospital with severe burns. Later, he was assigned to 32 GIAP, but was prevented from flying dangerous missions. In 1943 he was transferred back to 12 GIAP of the Moscow Air Defence zone, where he spent the rest of the war with little opportunity to see real combat.

Meanwhile, Timur Frunze went to 161 IAP. He flew only nine sorties before being shot down and killed over Staraya Russa on 19 January 1942, apparently after being credited with two shared victories.

In late summer 1942 Vladimir Mikoyan was assigned to 434 IAP (soon to become 32 GIAP), which was operating with 8 Air Army at Stalingrad. But he too lasted only a couple of weeks and was shot down and killed after only a few sorties and a single victory.

Leonid Khrushchev had competed 27 missions flying the SB bomber during July 1941 before he was shot down, breaking his leg in the crash-landing. After his release from hospital he transferred to fighters, and at the end of 1942 he was sent to 18 GIAP, then flying the Yak-7B. Khrushchev proved himself a superior pilot in training, but within days of entering combat he was shot down by a Fw 190 and killed.

Valentin Yaroslavskii and Lev Bulganin were eventually assigned to 12 GIAP, safely based in the rear with Stepan Mikoyan. Although the sons of the Soviet elite were brave, and several were highly skilled, the system was intent on protecting them from themselves.

A particularly special group of Yak pilots were the women of 586 IAP, one of three all-female regiments. Much romance and mythology has been attached to these pilots and, indeed, women had played a notable role in Russian aviation from the very start. Several progressive young women became fliers even before 1914, and it is said that at least one managed to fly a few missions with the Imperial Air Corps.

When the Soviets came to power women assumed an even bigger role. They played an active and significant part in the aero club movement of the 1930s, and many of the country's parachuting and flying instructors were women. Some, like Valentina Grizodubova, Polina Osipenko and Marina Raskova, made daring long-distance flights during the 1930s, while others achieved fame for aerobatic flying. There were even one or two who flew in Air Force units.

So, when Marina Raskova approached Stalin with a proposal to form a division of women fliers, the real novelty for the Soviets was not so much the idea of women combat pilots, but of deploying them in significant numbers and organising them in special all-women regiments. It was precisely the novelty of the proposal that appealed to Stalin, and he quickly gave his approval. The women's division was organised in mid 1942, and comprised 586 IAP, 587 BAP (Bomber Air Regiment), flying the Pe-2, and 588 NBAP (Night Bomber Air Regiment) with Po-2 night bombers.

Although Raskova had dreamed of the regiments fighting together at the front as a division, their different equipment made this unrealistic, and the regiments were deployed separately. Yak-1-equipped 586 IAP was based at Saratov from August 1942 as a PVO interceptor unit.

Unfortunately, the unit CO, Maj Kazarinova, was both a difficult person and a poor commander who drove the regiment to a state of near mutiny.

Lilya Litvyak, Katya Budanova and Mariya Kuznetsova plan a mission (*G F Petrov*)

Eventually, in October 1942, she was relieved of command and transferred to a headquarters position in Moscow. But before then, on 10 September, one of the regiment's squadrons had been disbanded and eight pilots – those considered the best in the regiment – were transferred to male regiments at the front. Snr Lt Raisa Belyaeva's flight, containing sergeant pilots Ekaterina Budanova, Mariya Kuznetsova and Lilya Litvyak, was sent to 437 IAP, while Capts Antonina Lebedeva, Klavdiya Blinova, Klavdiya Nechaeva and Olga Shakhova went to 434 IAP to form the Lebedeva flight.

When Maj Kazarinova was relieved of command, she was replaced by Maj Aleksandr Gridnev, a man with a troubled past that included two run-ins with the Secret Police and a term in the GULAG during the 1930s! Initially, he too got off to a bad start with 'his girls', but eventually they came to treasure him. But Gridnev's arrival marked the end of 586 IAP as an all-women regiment. Men also became deputy commanders, and when a third squadron was re-established in 1943, male pilots were assigned to it. Later 586 IAP received Yak-7s and Yak-9s and was eventually assigned to Front PVO, advancing into Austria by the end of the war.

During the conflict 586 IAP flew a total of 4419 sorties and scored 38 kills for the loss of ten pilots. Of those victories, five individual and two group kills were credited to Gridnev, who was the only pilot to qualify as an ace with 586 IAP. The regiment's top-scoring woman appears to have been Raisa Surnachevskaya with three individual victories, plus one shared.

The only fair conclusion is that this regiment served honourably but without distinction. For success we must consider the pilots who departed in September 1942.

Lilya Litvyak poses for the camera in her winter flying overall and fur-lined flying boots in early 1943 (*T Heffner*)

The Lebedeva flight did not last long. Lt Nechaeva managed to complete five sorties and score a single victory before she was shot down and killed on 17 September 1942. Soon afterward, Lebedeva, Blinova and Shakhova were transferred to 653 IAP (later 65 GIAP). Lebedeva scored three victories before being shot down and killed on 17 July 1943, while Klavdiya Blinova flew 156 sorties and claimed one individual and one group victory prior to being downed on 4 August 1943. A week later she succeeded in escaping, together with a number of other prisoners, and returned to the Soviet lines. After being vetted by SMERSh, she was allowed to return to duty, but was sent to a command school and did not see combat again. Olga Shakhova managed to survive 144 sorties, although without scoring any victories.

Lt Belyaeva's flight stayed only briefly with La-5-equipped 437 IAP before being sent to 9 GIAP, flying Yak-1s. But its CO, leading ace

Lev Shestakov, believed women had no place in combat. Raisa Belyaeva did little to change her new CO's point of view when she got herself shot down within days of arriving in the frontline while apparently on a training mission. When she was released from hospital, Belyaeva returned to 586 IAP. The two remaining women pilots, Budanova and Litvyak, were quickly transferred out of the regiment.

They were next assigned to 296 IAP (later 73 GIAP), and again their initial reception was not favorable. Col Baranov was persuaded to accept them only by Aleksei Salomatin – one of his best pilots who eventually became an ace with 17 individual and 22 shared victories, as well as a HSU.

**Top and above**
**Two more views of the well photographed Lilya Litvyak. These shots were taken in early 1943, by which time she had become an ace with 296 IAP (*T Heffner*)**

After proving their skills, Lilya and Katya often flew on the wing for Salomatin and Baranov, and won their places in the regiment. Litvyak was a particularly skilled pilot who insisted on celebrating each kill by beating up the aerodrome, even though this was strictly forbidden. Upon landing, she would coyly ask her mechanic, 'Did our father shout at me?' Lilya was respected by all. But to one pilot she was particularly special, for she and Salomatin soon fell in love.

On 15 March 1943 Lilya was wounded in the leg in air combat, but she kept on fighting and shot down two bombers. She passed out through loss of blood soon after landing, and was hospitalised until May. Just days before she returned to 73 GIAP, her fiancé Salomatin crashed fatally while testing a repaired Yak. She was wounded a second time on 16 July, and one week later she was flying with the new regimental CO when they were attacked by ten Bf 109s. Maj Golyshev was killed and Lilya was wounded a third time and had to take to her parachute.

On 1 August she shot down a Bf 109, but vanished into the cloud and was not seen again. She had flown 168 sorties and was credited with 11 aircraft and one balloon shot down, plus three shared victories. Since rumours persisted of a blonde woman fighter pilot in German captivity, Litvyak's nomination for the HSU was rejected. Only in 1989 was her body found, and in May 1990 President Mikhail Gorbachev finally awarded her a posthumous HSU.

For some reason Katya Budanova never received the publicity of her friend Lilya Litvyak, but she was just as deserving, and as excellent a pilot. On 19 June 1943 she was shot down over Voroshilovgrad while escorting bombers, whose crews confirmed that she shot down two Fw 190s in her last fight. Budanova flew 256 sorties and was officially credited with 20 victories, although that does not seem to include her final two kills. Like Litvyak, she was denied the HSU until her body was found in 1988. In October 1993 President Boris Yeltsin awarded her a posthumous Hero of Russia award.

# APPENDICES

## Fighter Regiments Identified as Operating Yaks

### Yak-1 Units

#### Guards Fighter Regiments

1, 9, 12, 14, 16, 18, 21, 26, 27, 29, 31, 32, 35, 38, 41, 42, 53, 54, 55, 56, 73, 84, 86, 89, 103, 106, 112, 116, 117, 139, 146, 148, 152, 153, 156 and 168 GIAPs

#### Fighter Regiments

2, 4, 6, 7, 8, 9, 10, 11, 12, 13, 14, 15, 16,17, 18, 20, 24, 25, 26, 27, 32, 34, 42, 43, 45, 49, 66, 91, 92, 117, 120, 121, 122, 123, 126, 127, 146, 148, 149, 153, 157, 158, 161, 162, 163, 165, 168, 170, 171, 172, 176, 179, 182, 183, 184, 186, 188, 189, 211, 233, 234, 236, 237, 239, 246, 247, 248, 249, 254, 265, 267, 270, 271, 272, 273, 274, 283, 286, 287, 291, 293, 296, 298, 347, 355, 402, 416, 423, 425, 427, 429, 431, 434, 438, 482, 484, 485, 487, 494, 508, 512, 513, 515, 516, 517, 518, 519, 520, 521, 536, 562, 563, 572, 573, 580, 581, 582, 586, 611, 628, 629, 651, 653, 659, 721, 722, 737, 739, 744, 745, 753, 754, 760, 767, 768, 769, 774, 787, 788, 805, 812, 814, 821, 827, 831, 832, 845, 866, 867, 875, 876, 894, 895, 896, 897, 900, 907, 910, 929, 964, 976 and Normandie IAPs

#### Naval Regiments

2 GIAP-SF, 3 GIAP-KBF, 6 GIAP-ChF, 10 GIAP-KBF, 14 GIAP-KBF, 7 IAP-ChF, 8 IAP-ChF, 9 IAP-ChF, 12 IAP-KBF, 13 IAP-KBF, 20 IAP-SF, 21 IAP-KBF, 25 IAP-ChF, 32 IAP-ChF, 62 IAP-ChF, 71 IAP-KBF and 255 IAP-SF

### Yak-7 Units

#### Guards Fighter Regiments

1, 9, 12, 18, 29, 31, 32, 42, 56, 64, 66, 72, 73, 84, 86, 89, 106, 107, 115, 117, 146, 148, 153 and 168 GIAPs

#### Fighter Regiments

4, 5, 6, 8, 12, 20, 27, 32, 41, 42, 43, 50, 91, 120, 127, 133, 146, 149, 152, 157, 159, 162, 163, 167, 168, 172, 183, 195, 236, 248, 254, 265, 267, 270, 271, 273, 283, 287, 291, 296, 315, 383, 402, 415, 427, 431, 434, 438, 439, 482, 484, 485, 487, 508, 512, 513, 515, 517, 518, 519, 520, 554, 582, 586, 611, 628, 630, 728, 737, 744, 761, 767, 768, 769, 774, 787, 788, 812, 814, 827, 831, 832, 845, 866, 867, 875, 896, 897, 910, 926, 938, 960, 964, 975 and 976 IAPs

#### Naval Regiments

4 GIAP-KBF, 6 GIAP-ChF, 10 GIAP-KBF, 11 GIAP-ChF, 14 GIAP-KBF, 7 IAP-ChF, 12 IAP-KBF, 13 IAP-KBF, 20 IAP-SF, 21 IAP-KBF and 25 IAP-ChF

## Yak-9 Units

### Guards Fighter Regiments

1,12,14,18, 26, 27, 29, 32, 42, 53, 54, 55, 56, 64, 65, 66, 73, 84, 85, 86, 89, 103,106, 112, 115, 117, 133, 139, 146, 148, 149, 150, 151, 152 and 156 GIAPs

### Fighter Regiments

4, 5, 12, 15, 20, 32, 34, 41, 42, 43, 122, 127, 133, 146, 148, 149, 157, 162, 163, 168, 179, 195, 197, 246, 248, 254, 265, 267, 269, 270, 274, 287, 291, 293, 300, 307, 347, 352, 368, 369, 402, 404, 409, 427, 431, 434, 483, 512, 515, 518, 554, 581, 582, 586, 611, 659, 728, 761, 767, 774, 781, 802, 812, 827, 832, 845, 847, 866, 867, 897, 900, 907, 909, 910, 940, 961, 976 and Normandie IAPs

### Naval Regiments

2 GIAP-SF, 6 GIAP-ChF, 14 GIAP-KBF, 12 IAP-KBF, 13 IAP-KBF, 14 IAP-TOF, 16 IAP-TOF, 19 IAP-TOF, 20 IAP-SF, 21 IAP-KBF, 38 IAP-TOF, 42 IAP-TOF, 59 IAP-TOF and 61 IAP-TOF

## Yak-9U Units

### Guards Fighter Regiments

29, 42, 133, 139 and 151 GIAPs

### Fighter Regiments

149, 163, 483, 515, 812 IAPs

### Naval Regiment

6 GIAP-ChF

## Yak-3 Units

### Guards Fighter Regiments

1, 18, 31, 56, 64, 65, 66, 67, 85, 86,112, 115, 116, 133, 148, 149, 150, 151, 152 and 153 GIAPs

### Fighter Regiments

15, 35, 43, 66, 91, 133, 157, 162, 176, 233, 274, 291, 347, 402, 431, 515, 554, 611, 659, 787, 812, 866, 876, 897, 900, 910 and Normandie IAPs

### Abbreviations

| | |
|---|---|
| HSU | Hero of the Soviet Union |
| IAP | Fighter Aviation Regiment |
| IAD | Fighter Aviation Division |
| G | Guards |
| -ChF | Black Sea Fleet |
| -KBF | Red Banner Baltic Fleet |
| -SF | Northern Fleet |
| -TOF | Pacific Ocean Fleet |

## Top-Scoring Soviet Yak Pilots

| Name | Rank | Award | Unit | Victories (Individual & Shared) |
|---|---|---|---|---|
| Vorozheikin, Arsenii Vasil'ovich | Maj | 2 x HSU | 728 IAP | 52 & 13 |
| Koldunov, Aleksandr Ivanovich | Capt | 2 x HSU | 866 IAP | 46 & 1 |
| Alelyukhin, Aleksei Vasil'evich | Maj | 2 x HSU | 9 GIAP | 40 & 17 |
| Luganskii, Sergei Danilovich | Maj | 2 x HSU | 152 GIAP | 38 & 6 |
| Murav'yov, Pavel Ignat'evich | Capt | HSU | 64 GIAP | 37 & 5 |
| Lavrinenkov, Vladimir Dmitrievich | Maj | 2 x HSU | 9 GIAP | 36 & 11 |
| Reshetov, Aleksei Mikhailovich | Maj | HSU | 31 GIAP | 36 & 8 |
| Fyodorov, Ivan Vasil'evich | Snr Lt | HSU | 812 IAP | 36 & 1 |
| Pavlushkin, Nikolai Sazonovich | Snr Lt | HSU | 402 IAP | 35 & 48? |
| Kochetov, Aleksandr Vasil'evich | Capt | HSU | 43 IAP | 34 & 8 |
| Stepanenko, Ivan Nikiforovich | Maj | 2 x HSU | 4 IAP | 33 & 8 |
| Borovykh, Andrei Egorovich | Maj | 2 x HSU | 157 IAP | 32 & 14 |
| Chirkov, Andrei Vasil'evich | Maj | HSU | 29 GIAP | 32 & 9 |
| Ryazanov, Aleksei Konstantinovich | Maj | 2 x HSU | 4 IAP | 31 & 16 |
| Pokryshev, Pyotr Afanas'evich | Lt Col | 2 x HSU | 154 IAP | 31 & 7 |
| Amet-Khan, Sultan | Maj | 2 x HSU | 9 GIAP | 30 & 19 |
| Makarov, Valentin Nikolaevich | Maj | HSU | 53 GIAP | 30 & 9 |
| Denisenko, Vladimir Gur'evich | Snr Lt | HSU | 32 IAP | 30 |
| Churilin, Aleksei Pavlovich | Maj | HSU | 611 IAP | 30 & 21 |
| Shmelyov, Il'ia Vasil'evich | Maj | HSU | 4 IAP | 29 & 15 |
| Kiriya, Shalva Nestorovich | Maj | HSU | 151 GIAP | 29 & 2 |
| Merkushev, Vasilii Afanas'evich | Maj | HSU | 270 IAP | 29 |
| Romanenko, Ivan Ivanovich | Capt | HSU | 774 IAP | 28 & 1 |
| Kovzan, Boris Ivanovich | Lt Col | HSU | 744 IAP | 28 & 1 |
| Treshchev, Konstantin Mikhailovich | Capt | HSU | 127 IAP | 28 |
| Sivtsov, Nikolai Stepanovich | Snr Lt | HSU | 107 GIAP | 28 |
| Morgunov, Sergei Nikolaevich | Capt | HSU | 15 IAP | 27 & 16 |
| Safronov, Sergei Ivanovich | Maj | HSU | 293 IAP | 27 & 4 |

| Name | Rank | Award | Unit | Victories (Individual & Shared) |
|---|---|---|---|---|
| Grishchenko, Pyotr Luk'yanovich | Lt | HSU | 32 IAP | 27 & 1 balloon |
| Kharitonov, Vasilii Nikolaevich | Snr Lt | HSU | 123 IAP | 26 & 11 |
| Baranov, Mikhail Semyonovich | Maj | HSU | 157 IAP | 26 & 9 |
| Naidyonov, Nikolai Alekseevich | Snr Lt | HSU | 563 IAP | 26 & 3 |
| Lavrenov, Aleksandr Filippovich | Capt | HSU | 291 IAP | 26 & 3 |
| Sachkov, Mikhail Ivanovich | Capt | HSU | 728 IAP | 26 |
| Popov, Ivan Feoktistovich | Lt Col | - | 812 IAP | 26 |
| Pivovarov, Mikhail Evdokimovich | Snr Lt | HSU | 402 IAP | 26 |
| Didenko, Gavriil Vlasovich | Maj | HSU | 482 IAP | 25 & 37 |
| Suvirov, Viktor Ivanovich | Maj | HSU | 15 IAP | 25 & 7 |
| Klimov, Vasilii Vladimirovich | Maj | HSU | 15 IAP | 25 & 2 |
| Yashin, Viktor Nikolaevich | Capt | HSU | 133 IAP | 25 |
| Manukyan, Akop Balabekovich | Capt | HSU | 402 IAP | 25 |
| Baranov, Mikhail Dmitrievich | Snr Lt | HSU | 183 IAP | 24 & 28 |
| Dunaev , Nikolai Panteleevich | Capt | HSU | 152 GIAP | 24 & 9 |
| Morozov, Anatolii Afanas'evich | Maj | HSU | 4 IAP | 24 & 8 |
| Zudilov, Ivan Sergeevich | Capt | HSU | 163 IAP | 24 & 6 |
| Osadchiev, Aleksandr Dmitrievich | Capt | HSU | 43 IAP | 24 & 6 |
| Nagornii, Viktor Sergeevich | Snr Lt | HSU | 293 IAP | 24 & 6 |
| Pogorelov, Mikhail Savel'evich | Capt | HSU | 4 IAP | 24 & 5 |
| Somov, Ivan Konstantinovich | Capt | HSU | 86 GIAP | 24 & 4 |
| Gorbunov, Ivan Mikhailovich | Lt | HSU | 42 GIAP | 24 & 3 |
| Bastrikov, Aleksandr Mikhailovich | Capt | - | 15 IAP | 24 & 2 |
| Vakhlaev, Aleksandr Alekseevich | Capt | HSU | 728 IAP | 24 |
| Motuz, Ivan Fomich | Capt | HSU | 86 GIAP | 24 |
| Kornienko, Ivan Mikheevich | Capt | HSU | 152 GIAP | 24 |
| Ashchaulov, Dmitrii Nikolaevich | Capt | - | 402 IAP | 24 |

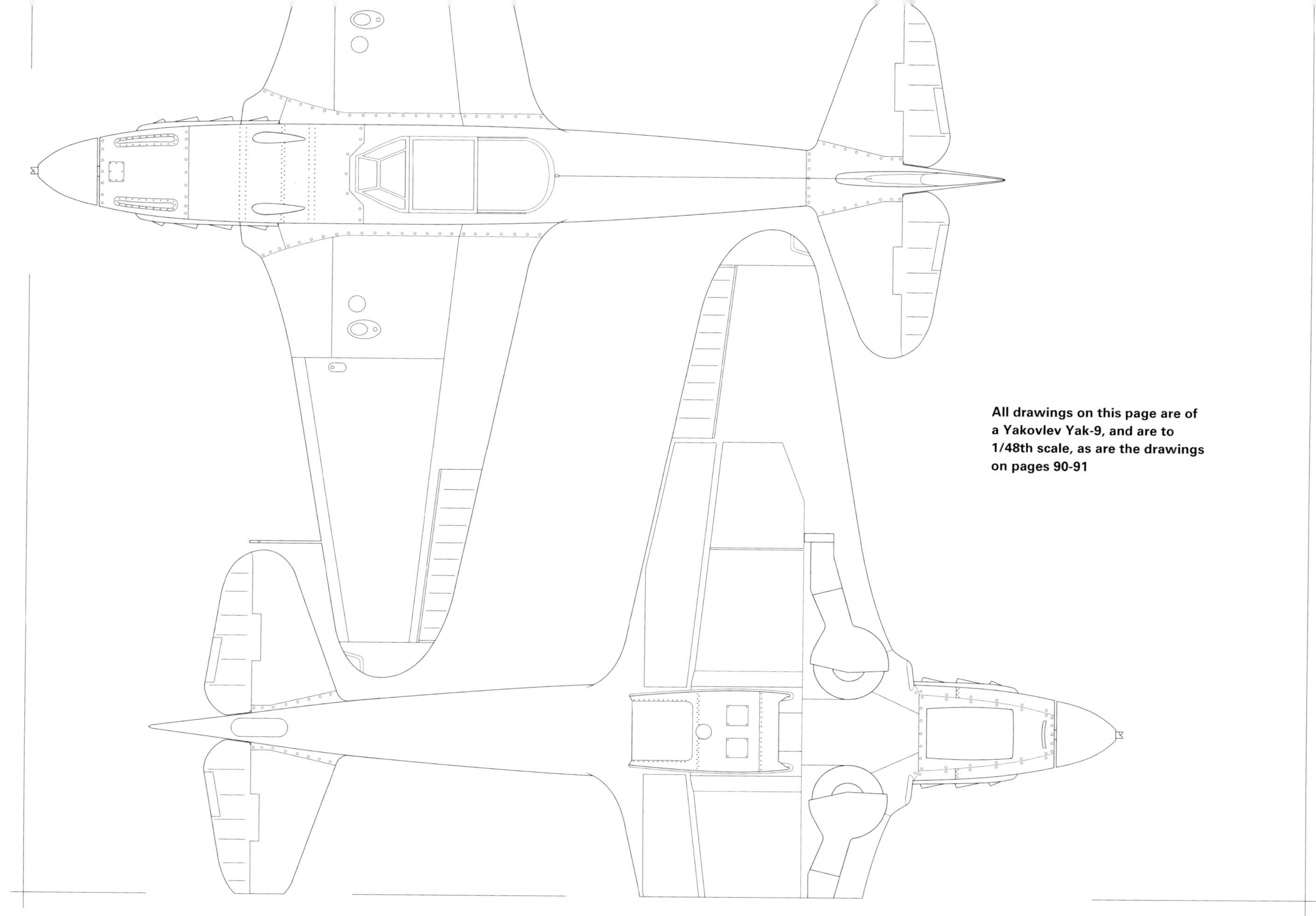

**All drawings on this page are of a Yakovlev Yak-9, and are to 1/48th scale, as are the drawings on pages 90-91**

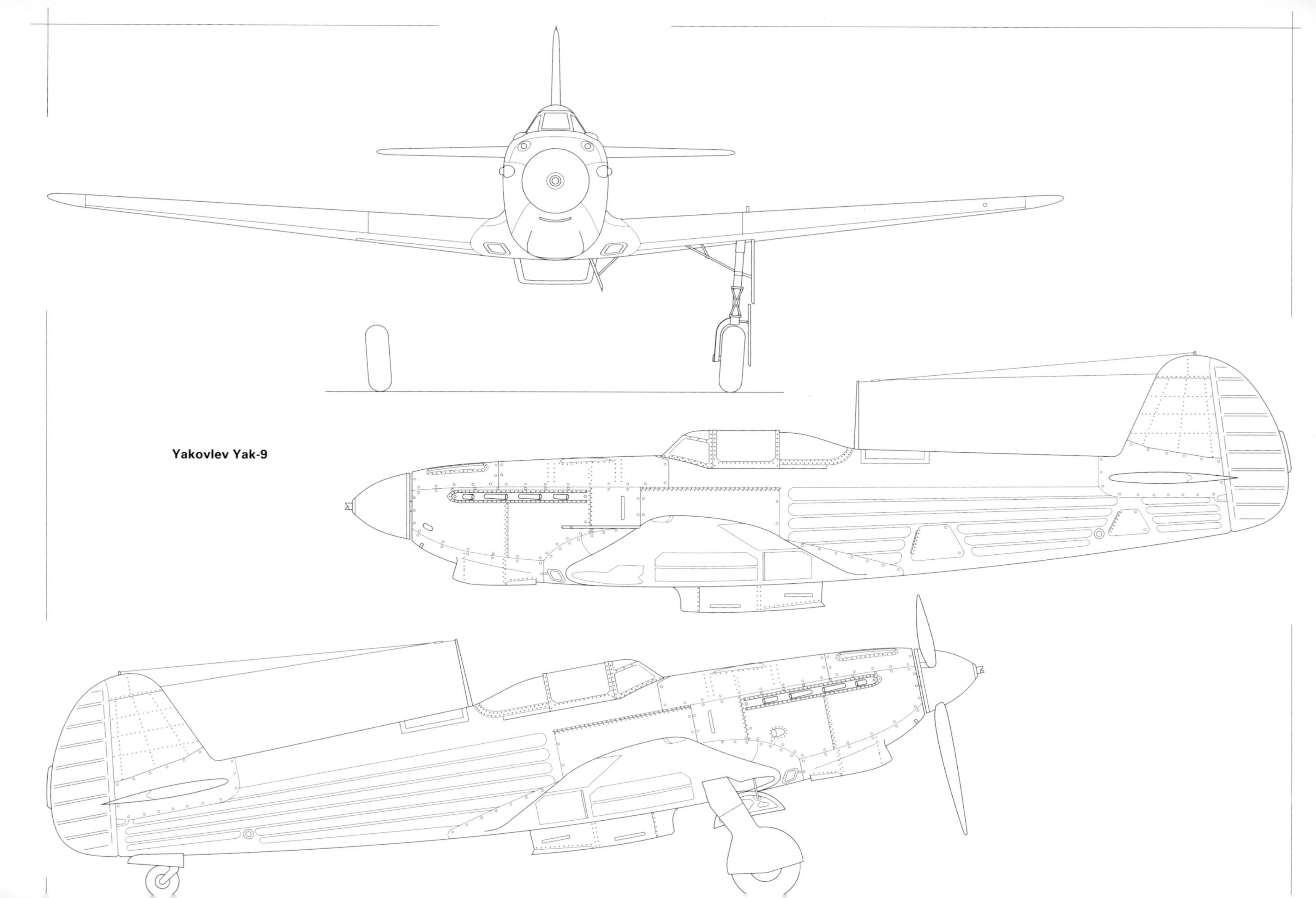
Yakovlev Yak-9

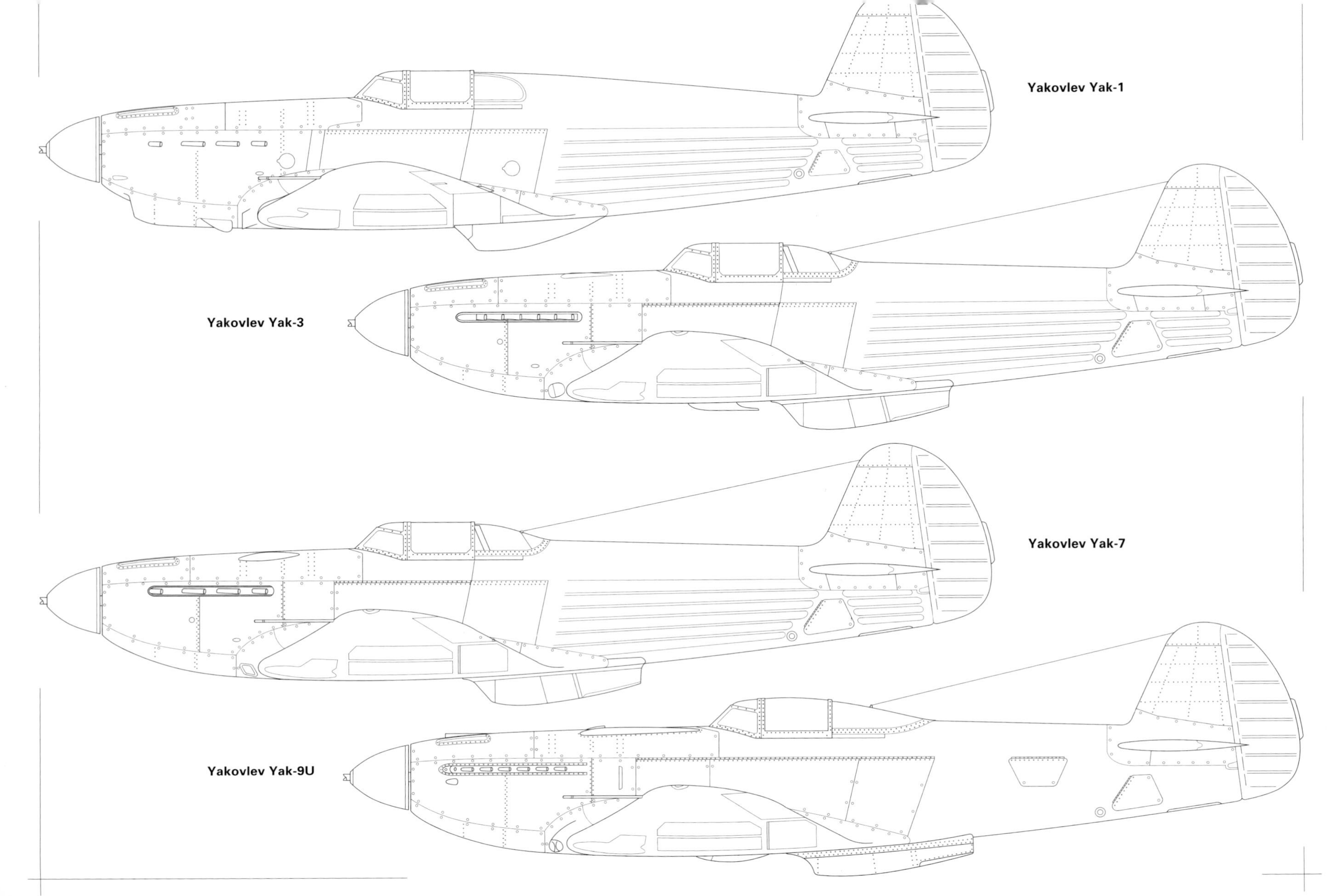
Yakovlev Yak-1
Yakovlev Yak-3
Yakovlev Yak-7
Yakovlev Yak-9U

## COLOUR PLATES

### 1

**Yak-1 of Snr Lt Mikhail Dmitrievich Baranov, 183 IAP, South-western Front, summer 1942**

This aircraft has standard green and black uppersurfaces and light blue undersurfaces, with its stars outlined in black. Displayed behind the cockpit are 24 victory stars and the slogan *Groza Fashchistov M D Baranov* (*M D Baranov, Terror of the Fascists*).

### 2

**Yak-1 of Capt Boris Nikolaevich Eryomin, 296 IAP, South-western Front, winter 1941-42**

This fighter was delivered from the factory with skis and white camouflage. Ski-equipped Yak-1s which survived the winter were probably sent to a rear maintenance base in the spring for conversion to wheeled landing gear and repainting in regular camouflage. This was probably the aircraft in which Eryomin fought in the famous 'battle of seven against 25' on 9 March 1942.

### 3

**Yak-1 of Snr Lt Innokentii Vasil'evich Kuznetsov, 180 IAP, Kalinin Front, March 1942**

This aircraft is noteworthy for the combination of white and red victory stars behind the cockpit on an unpainted section of green and black camouflage. Such coloured stars usually differentiated individual from unit victories. Kuznetsov ended the war with an official score of 15 individual and 12 shared victories, yet despite this success he did not receive the HSU until March 1991.

### 4

**Yak-1B (serial 08110) of Maj Boris Nikolaevich Eryomin, 31 GIAP, Stalingrad Front, December 1942**

This was the first aircraft donated to the VVS by Ferapont Golovatii. The left side displays, in red, the inscription *Iyotchiky Stalingradskogo fronta Gvardii Maioru tv. Eryominy ot kholkhoznika kholkhoz 'stakanovets' tv. Golovatoga* (*To the aviator of the Stalingrad Front Guards Major comrade Eryomin, from a collective farmer of the 'Stakhanovets' Collective Farm, comrade Golovatii*). On the right side was the legend *Stalingradskomy fronty ot kholkhoznika kholkhoz 'stakanovets' tv. Golovatoga* (*To the Stalingrad Front from a collective farmer of the 'Stakhanovets' Collective Farm, comrade Golovatii*). The fighter also featured a row of seven red victory stars on its starboard side.

### 5

**Yak-1B (serial 08110) of Maj Boris Nikolaevich Eryomin, 31 GIAP, Stalingrad Front, summer 1943**

Eryomin's long-lived Yak-1B 08110 is seen here stripped of its white winter finish, and with the donation inscription carefully reapplied over its summer green and black camouflage. Note the diagonal red on fighter's fin and rudder. Such bands in various colours appear to have been a common Soviet formation marking throughout the war. By the summer of 1944 this aircraft had exceeded its permitted flying hours, and when Eryomin received a new one, it was put on public display in Saratov, where it had been built.

### 6

**Yak-1B of Maj Aleksei Mikhailovich Reshetov, 31 GIAP, 4 Ukrainian Front, autumn 1943**

This aircraft displays the legend *Kholkozniki Shatovskogo s/soveta Shatovskogo r-na Zaporozhskoi obl. Geroyu Sovetskogo Soyuza Gvardii Maioru Reshetovu* (*From the collective farmers of the Shatovskii rural council, Shatovskii region, Zaporozh'e District, to Guards Major Reshetov*). The use of dark green in the uppersurface camouflage of this machine was unusual by late 1943. Indeed, some Russian sources have described this aircraft as wearing standard dark and light grey late war camouflage.

### 7

**Yak-1B of Lt Lilya Vladimirovna Litvyak, 296 IAP, South Front, summer 1943**

Famous female fighter pilot Lilya Litvyak primarily flew straight-backed Yak-1 'Yellow 44' during her brief combat career with 296 IAP. However, she was issued with this newly built Yak-1B in the early summer of 1943.

### 8

**Yak-1B of Capt Nikolai Aleksandrovich Kozlov, 910 IAP (PVO unit), Borisoglebsk, February 1943**

Before converting to the Yak-1, Kozlov had flown MiG-3s, and by war's end he was a major commanding a Lavochkin-equipped regiment. During the conflict he scored at least 19 individual and five shared victories, including two by ramming. About half of these were achieved with the Yak-1. The fighter's white spinner was a regimental marking unique to 910 IAP at this time.

### 9

**Yak-1B of Snr Lt V F Korobov, 34 IAP, Moscow PVO Zone, spring 1943**

Few details have emerged about V F Korobov's combat career, although it is believed that he scored at least 18 victories.

### 10

**Yak-1B of Capt Vladimir Pavlovich Pokrovskii, 2 GIAP-SF, Northern Fleet, late 1943**

Pokrovskii had flown I-16s, Hurricanes and Kittyhawks in the immediate aftermath of Germany's invasion of the USSR. Having survived the carnage of 1941-42, he was issued with a Yak-1B and ended the war with 12 individual and six shared victories to his credit. It is not known if Pokrovskii's unique personal markings appeared on both sides of the fuselage of his colourful Yak-1B.

### 11

**Yak-1B of Maj Sergei Danilovich Luganskii, 152 GIAP, 2 Ukrainian Front, May 1944**

This aircraft was purchased for Luganskii by his home city while he was there recovering from wounds in late 1943. The inscription reads *Geroyu Sovetskogo Soyuza Sergei Luganskomu ot Komsomoltsev i molodyomi g. Alma-Ata* (*To Hero of the Soviet Union Sergei Luganskii from the Komsomolists and youths of the city Alma-Ata*). The yellow number 32 indicated Luganskii's victory tally at the time of presentation.

## 12
**Yak-1B of Capt Pavel Maksimovich Chuvilev, CO 1st Squadron, 427 IAP, Kalinin Front, August 1943**
The fuselage inscription on this aircraft reads *ot trudyashchikhsya pugachevskogo r-na* (*From the workers of the Pugachev Region*). The red nose signified that this Yak-1B was flown by a member of the special *myech* (sword) group of dedicated hunters. The bands around the fuselage distinguished the regiment's aircraft from a captured example, believed to have been operated by the Luftwaffe in the same region, and as a result their appearance changed almost daily. Chuvilev ended the war as a colonel on the staff of 193 IAD, having flown 350 sorties and scored 15 individual and five shared victories.

## 13
**Yak-1B of Maj Yakov Nazarovich Kutikhin, Deputy CO and later CO of 247 IAP (156 GIAP from 5 February 1944), 1 and 2 Ukrainian Fronts, 1944**
Kutikhin flew this aircraft between February 1943 and September 1944. The Guards badge on the nose was displayed from February 1944, and the light and dark green finish is unusual for Yak-1s. Also unusual is the replacement of the aircraft number with a personal marking on the right side of the fuselage (see scrap view). Kutikhin flew 303 sorties and fought in 56 air combats, scoring eight individual and two shared victories, plus four more aircraft destroyed on the ground.

## 14
**Yak-1B of Snr Lt Aleksandr Alekseevich Shokurov, 2nd Squadron, 156 GIAP, Poland 1944**
The medium blue spinner on this aircraft, which Shokurov flew until the end of the war, is probably a squadron marking. He scored his first victory on 2 June 1942, and completed 460 sorties and claimed 18 individual kills, plus one shared, in 60 air combats.

## 15
**Yak-7B of Maj Andrei Vasil'evich Chirkov, 29 GIAP, Leningrad Front, Summer 1943**
Chirkov flew this aircraft during the spring of 1943. While Russian references depict this aircraft as finished in two shades of green, it is also possible that the colours could have been green and black, as both camouflage schemes were used on the Yak-7 in 1943. The insignia on the fuselage is the Guards badge.

## 16
**Yak-7B of Capt Viktor Yakovlevich Khasin, 271 IAP, Kalinin Front, spring 1943**
The yellow bands on the fuselage, tail and beneath the wings of this aircraft served as identification markings. The display of crossed-out swastikas as victory markings is highly unusual, and has been observed only among aircraft operated by 271 and 875 IAPs of 274 IAD, as well as 42 IAP. Khasin was killed in action on 14 January 1944 after flying more than 700 sorties and scoring 13 individual and five shared victories in 300 air combats. He is credited with destroying another eight enemy aircraft on the ground, and was awarded the HSU on 1 May 1943.

## 17
**Yak-7A of 12 GIAP, Moscow PVO Zone, June 1942**
The inscription displayed on this aircraft reads *Komsomol Kuzbassa* (*Kuzbass Komsomol*). An entire squadron of aircraft was contributed to the regiment by Komsomol, the communist Youth league. Each was marked in the same style with the name of a different regional organisation. Number 5 was *Komsomol Kolymy*, and Number 9 was *Novosibirskii Komsomol*, which also featured a broad red arrow painted over the engine exhausts. The specific pilots to which these aircraft were assigned remain unknown.

## 18
**Yak-7B of Capt Pyotr Afanas'evich Pokryshev, 29 GIAP, Leningrad Front, summer 1943**
This aircraft was flown by Pokryshev during the spring and summer of 1943. Later, in 1944-45, it was exhibited in the Defence of Leningrad Museum. Compared with the Yak-7B in Profile 15, this aircraft uses the common green and black camouflage. It was not uncommon for aircraft to sport different camouflage schemes in the same regiment at the same time.

## 19
**Yak-7B of Capt Vladimir Ivanovich Merkulov, 43 IAP/3 IAK, September 1943**
Merkulov sometimes flew as wingman for Gen Savitskii, and on one occasion, while flying this aircraft, he shielded the general from attack by flying between the attacker and Savitskii, who escaped. Merkulov completed 250 sorties and scored 21 individual and four shared victories. He was awarded the HSU on 26 October 1944. This aircraft displays the distinctive insignia which Savitskii selected for his corps, as well as the fuselage inscription *For Nikolai*, commemorating a fallen friend.

## 20
**Yak-7B of Snr Sgt Pavel Petrovich Karavai, 897 IAP, late December 1942**
Karavai flew this aircraft between late October 1942 and February 1943, during which time he used it to score 16 victories. By the end of the war Karavai was a captain and had completed 232 sorties. Officially, he was credited with 16 individual and seven shared victories, but unofficially he scored 31 individual and seven shared kills. Karavai was awarded the HSU on 18 August 1945. The inscription on the side reads *ishchu* (*I search*). The personal markings seen on this Yak, were repeated on both sides of the fuselage.

## 21
**Yak-7B of Jnr Lt Evgenii Mikhailovich Shutov, 29 GIAP, North-west Front, late 1943**
This aircraft was damaged in combat on 25 January 1944 and the Ace of Spades insignia just forward of the tail unit was over-painted at the repair depot. It was damaged again in a

forced landing on 7 February 1944 and written off. Aside from the Spade, the Yak also boasted an unusual orange spinner and rudder. Shutov scored five individual victories in about 100 sorties.

### 22
**Yak-9 of Snr Lt Ivan Nikiforovich Stepanenko, 4 IAP, Bryansk, July 1943**

Stepanenko was allocated this aircraft in June 1943 and flew it until he received a Yak-9T. The Yak-9's artwork, painted by his mechanic, depicted a springing tiger attacking Nazi propaganda minister Joseph Goebbels, who is fleeing in terror with his microphone. Some sources represent this aircraft as displaying late war dark and light grey camouflage, but that is incorrect, as the black and green scheme was still in use when the aircraft was delivered in 1943. Indeed, field units were ordered not to bother spending time repainting the camouflage. The crest of the Order of the Red Banner would have appeared on the nose from 5 November 1944, when 4 IAP was awarded that distinction. After Stepanenko received his Yak-9T, this aircraft was flown by 44-kill ace Il'ya Vasil'evich Shmelyov.

### 23
**Yak-7B of Capt Arsenii Vasil'evich Vorozheikin, 728 IAP, Kiev, November 1943**

On 5 November 1943 Vorozheikin and several other pilots painted the noses of their Yaks red to celebrate the imminent liberation of Kiev and the forthcoming anniversary of the 1917 Revolution. At the end of November Vorozheikin exchanged the aircraft for a new Yak-9D. He removed the sliding canopies from all of his aircraft after suffering a damaged canopy in action on 14 July 1943 which hampered his escape from his burning Yak-7.

### 24
**Yak-9 of Maj Aleksandr Nikolaevich Kiloberidze, 65 GIAP, Latvia, October 1944**

This aircraft has often been associated with the apparently fictitious six-kill ace Vano T Gugridze, but photographs clearly show A N Kiloberidze to be its pilot. He served with 65 GIAP and scored at least 15 victories before being killed in a mid-air collision over Latvia in October 1944. The inscription under the canopy reads *za brata Shota* (*For brother Shota*), while the titling on the arrow says *na zapad* (*To the west*).

### 25
**Yak-9 of Capt Nikolai Fyodorovich Denchik, 64 GIAP, Belorussia, early 1944**

Denchik flew this aircraft from autumn 1943 until late 1944, when he received a dedication Yak-3 in its place. The inscription *Za Rodinu* (*For the Motherland*) was repeated on both sides of the fuselage.

### 26
**Yak-9 of Maj Abrek Arkad'evich Barsht, 118 OKRAP, 1 Ukrainian Front, late 1944**

Barsht completed 365 sorties and scored eight individual victories, including a Fw 190D shot down at the end of 1944, while flying with 118 OKRAP (*Otdel'nyi Korrektirovochnyi Razvedyvatel'nyi Aviatsionnyi Polk* – Separate Artillery Reconnaissance Air Regiment). He duly received the HSU on 10 April 1945.

### 27
**Yak-9D of Snr Lt Mikhail Ivanovich Grib, 6 GIAP-ChF, Crimea, May 1944**

Probably the most famous Yak fighter of them all thanks to a series of excellent in-flight photographs taken in 1944, this aircraft displays both the Guards and Order of the Red Banner emblems on its nose, as well as small victory symbols around the tail insignia.

### 28
**Yak-9D of Lt Col Mikhail Vasil'evich Avdeev, 6 GIAP-ChF, Crimea, May 1944**

As the regimental CO, Avdeev chose to substitute an easily-recognisable personal emblem for the standard side number. Also noteworthy on this aircraft is the unusual positioning of the 15 victory symbols around the tail insignia.

### 29
**Yak-9T of Maj Ivan Nikiforovich Stepanenko, 4 IAP, 2 Baltic Front, December 1944**

Aside from featuring Stepanenko's considerable victory tally and his personal emblem, this aircraft also displays the crest of the Order of the Red Banner on the nose. Stepanenko received this award no fewer than four times.

### 30
**Yak-9T of Snr Lt Aleksandr Ivanovich Vybornov, 728 IAP, 2 Ukrainian Front, autumn 1944**

This aircraft was delivered in September 1944 and written off the following month after being hit by flak. The inscription reads *A I Vybornovu ot Kashirskikh shkolnikov* (*To A I Vybornov from the schoolchildren of Kashira*). The cost of the fighter construction (72,000 rubles) had been paid for by the residents of Vybornov's home town.

### 31
**Yak-9T of Snr Lt Dmitrii Dmitrievich Tormakhov, 267 IAP, Rumania, June 1944**

Having flown the LaGG-3 in combat from January 1943, Dmitrii Tormakhov received this Yak-9T in April 1944 following the re-equipment of his unit with Yakovlev fighters. Twelve aircraft inscribed *osvobozhdenyi Donbass* (*Liberated Donbass*) were assigned to Tormakhov's 3rd Squadron. By war's end Tormakhov had flown 366 sorties and scored 14 individual and two shared victories in 71 air combats. He had also destroyed two aircraft on the ground, but only one individual and two shared victories were claimed while flying the Yak-9T.

### 32
**Yak-9T of Capt Ivan Ivanovich Vetrov, 66 GIAP, 1 Baltic Front, early June 1944**

Vetrov flew 117 sorties and scored 12 victories in 32 air combats. The parallel bands on the tail denote 4 GIAD. Note the silver-painted victory stars.

### 33
**Yak-9K of 3 IAK, Poland, late 1944**

This aircraft illustrates another variation of the distinctive markings displayed by the regiments of Savitskii's fighter corps. Whether they denoted different regiments or were the choice of individual pilots is not clear.

### 34

**Yak-9U of Lt Boris Aleksandrovich Loginov, 29 GIAP, Karelian Front, February 1945**

Loginov joined 29 GIAP in early 1943, and by the end of the war he had flown 172 sorties and fought 36 air combats. He was officially credited with eight individual and six group victories, and gave away four more to his wingman. In early 1944 Leningrad's famed Vakhtangova Ballet contributed funds to buy four fighters, all of which were donated to 29 GIAP and marked *Vakhtangovets* on both sides.

### 35

**Yak-3 of Lt Savelii Vasil'evich Nosov, 150 GIAP, Czechoslovakia, early 1945**

Nosov arrived at the front in June 1943 and was selected for 4 IAK's special hunter squadron, whose members painted the noses of their fighters blood red. By the end of the war Nosov had flown 149 sorties and scored 16 individual victories, plus one shared, in 38 combats. He was awarded the HSU on 15 May 1946.

### 36

**Yak-3 of 402 IAP/3 IAK, Germany, early 1945**

The pilot of this aircraft remains unknown, but it may have been regimental CO Maj Anatolii Ermolaevich Rubakhin, who scored 20 victories and was awarded the HSU on 23 February 1945. The nose displays yet another variation of the 3 IAK insignia.

### 37

**Yak-3 of Maj Gen Georgii Nefyodovich Zakharov, Commander 303 IAD, East Prussia, early 1945**

This aircraft displays the standard dark and light grey camouflage of the period, as well as 303 IAD's lightning bolt insignia, the Order of the Red Banner on the nose and Zakharov's personal crest. The insignia honours one of Russia's most famous icons, St George the Victory-Bearer, patron saint of Moscow, Russia and, particularly, the Russian Army pre-1918 (and since 1991). This rendition evokes the crest of Moscow city. Of course, since the Communists were 'Godless', a Red Army soldier replaced the saint – rendered here in such a way so as to suggest that it was Georgii Zakharov himself on horseback! Previous artworks of this Yak-3 have represented the background colour variously as blue, yellow or red. Light blue is the most likely, however.

### 38

**Yak-3 of 18 GIAP, Poland, early 1945**

The bold lightning bolt was not exclusive to the Yak fighters of the French Normandie Regiment, as it was also the formation marking of 303 IAD. A variation was also worn by 9 GIAP's La-7s. The more ornate style of number adorning this machine identifies it as a 18 GIAP fighter, rather than a Normandie Yak-3.

### 39

**Yak-3 of Snr Lt Ivan Vasil'evich Maslov, 157 IAP, Germany, 1945**

This aircraft displays a nose inscription which reads *Kolkhoz Krasnyi Oktyabr* (*Red October Collective Farm*), thus denoting the source of the donations which paid for its construction. By the end of the war Maslov had flown 350 sorties and scored 22 individual and 19 shared victories in 100 air combats. He received the HSU on 1 July 1944.

### 40

**Yak-9U of Capt Mikhail Ivanovich Grib, 6 GIAP-ChF, 3 Ukrainian Front, early 1945**

In late 1944 Soviet fighters began to change from the previous standard camouflage of dark and light grey patches to an overall light grey finish on the uppersurfaces. Grib has retained his established aircraft number on his new Yak and chosen a more conventional location for his victory scoreboard. The four yellow stars probably denote shared victories and the red markings (some of them obscured by the wing) individual kills. The red and yellow-faceted star almost certainly represents his HSU.

# INDEX

References to illustrations are shown in **bold**. Colour Plates are shown with page numbers and caption locators in brackets.